PRAISE FOR

Kathryn Al

"*Love Will Find You* gives many wise and practical suggestions for preparing yourself to find your true spiritual partner, while avoiding the hazards of false and overly romantic belief."

—Maurie D. Pressman, MD, co-author, *Twin Souls*

"Kathryn's work is inspirational and practical. Her words take you by the hand and heart and empower you to forge a new path through the scary and intimidating 'singles forest.' Be open to the process and possibilities."

—Kitty Bartholomew, author and host of *Kitty Bartholomew: You're Home*

"Wise and wonderful. Kathryn sees deeply and guides with simple direction. She is the best kind of trail blazer."

—Chris Paine, director of *Who Killed the Electric Car?*

"Thanks to Kathryn's teachings and CDs, I've finally been able to let go of past loves that were still haunting me, and move on with my life and to new love. I feel lighter, freer, and more open and fearless about future relationships than ever before."

—Alexandria Brown, www.EzineQueen.com

"Kathryn's work is essential in creating your ideal relationship. She teaches about the process of releasing people, in order to attract those who are for our highest good. Kathryn shows us the way to manifest the love relationship of our dreams."

—Steve Viglione,
CEO of the I AM Foundation

"Plenty of Angelenos wear their best karma for facilitator Kathryn Alice's relationships workshops."

—*Los Angeles* magazine

About the Author

Kathryn Alice, RScP, is a well-known love guru who teaches in more than seven cities through the Learning Annex and at conferences nationwide. Based at the Agape Spiritual Center in Los Angeles, Kathryn directed the center's Crisis Support Team for six years. She has appeared on *Montel*, in *Seventeen* magazine, *Psychology Today*, and on "Single Talk," among her many media appearances. A graduate of Vanderbilt University, Kathryn has had numerous articles published on the subject of love and dating. Happily married to her own soulmate, Kathryn, her husband, Jon, and their four children live and work in Venice Beach, California.

Love Will Find You

Love Will Find You

9 Magnets to Bring
You and Your Soulmate Together

Kathryn Alice, RScP

Marlowe & Company
New York

Love Will Find You:
9 Magnets to Bring You and Your Soulmate Together

Published by
Marlowe & Company
An Imprint of Avalon Publishing Group, Incorporated
245 West 17th Street • 11th Floor
New York, NY 10011-5300

Library of Congress Cataloging-in-Publication Data

Alice, Kathryn.
Love will find you : 9 magnets to bring you and your soulmate together/ Kathryn Alice.
p. cm.
Includes bibliographical references and index.
ISBN-13: 978-1-56924-277-3
ISBN-10: 1-56924-277-1
1. Mate selection. 2. Soul mates. 3. Man-woman relationships. 4. Intimacy (Psychology) I. Title.

HQ801.A524 2006
646.7'7–dc22

2006022088

9 8 7 6 5 4 3 2

Designed by Maria E. Torres
Printed in the United States of America

For Jon–

my soulmate, my lover, my husband

Thank you for all the love you have brought into my life

and for your constant support.

I love you always.

Contents

Acknowledgments

I am grateful to so many people who have aided my journey in writing this book. First, I thank God for showing me my calling, making it such a wonderful one, and supporting me with guidance every day. Second, I thank my soulmate and husband, Jon Tompkins, for making these concepts more than just theoretical for me. Living in this world of love that you have cocreated with me is more than I ever could have dreamed of in my life. I thank my children, Calvin, Jon-Jon, Chris, and the baby, for their support and love. You open our hearts even further and enrich our lives in countless ways. I thank my mom, Virginia Williams; my dad, Charles Nanney; sister, Beth Nicholson; brother, David Nanney; and their families for their guidance and cheerleading. I give thanks for my husband's family, now my own, who are a rich bonus that I didn't expect from my soulmate: my mother-in-law, Jane Tompkins; sister-in-law, Christa; brother-in-law, Dave; and their families. Thanks to Teresa Delgado for her support of my children and our family.

I am especially grateful for my talented good friend Susan Brandner, editor extraordinaire and gifted writer in her own right. You have been with me all the way, Susan, and I am touched by how much you have helped me on this journey.

I also thank another good friend and writer, Victoria Clayton Alexander, for her editing and inspirational help as well as Sabrina Buchanek, director of the Agape Singles Ministry and my brilliant brainstorm partner.

My mentors in life have helped me to heal my own wounds and modeled for me how to lead, and I thank them: the Reverend Michael Beckwith, my pastor and the founder of my home base, the Agape Spiritual Center; and his wife, Rickie Byars Beckwith; Jill Ruesch-Lane, DC, whom I talk about in the book; the Reverend Joan Steadman and Lorene Belisama. Also, thanks to my two grandmothers and mentors, Hattie and Vilma, who are my angels even though they're no longer here with me on Earth. Special thanks to Della Reese for sharing her inspirational love story with me. Thank you to my helpers in my work through the years: Jem Porter, Donna Jean McHenry, Stephanie Dawn, RScP, Pankaj Sharma, and Bob Scullion.

Thank you to Howard Jay Rubin, RScP, healing practitioner and Kabbalah teacher, for helping me to develop the material on releasing old loves in chapter 5. I am grateful to my partners in teaching during my early workshop years, Wesnia Roth and Ingrid Elfver Ryan, both of whom have also been mentors to me. I am thankful for the friendship and professional support of Robert Quicksilver, director of the Conscious Life Expo. I'm grateful as well for the support of Scott Catamas, a colleague, friend and mentor. I thank Mark Ryan for his professional guidance. Thanks also to my colleague Angela Montano, RScP, for a wonderful quote about love that she found on a greeting card and that I have used for years.

I believe that soulmates exist in business, too. And I have been very blessed to find my soulmates in the publishing world: my literary agent, Stephanie Kip Rostan, who is sensitive, smart, and an intuitive businessperson. I had so much fun running around New York with you, meeting with publishers, and I appreciate your extraordinary editing, guidance, and business gifts. Thanks to Stephanie's agency, Levine Greenberg, for their invaluable legal, business, and clerical expertise. Thanks to my editor, Renee Sedliar, for your support, your wonderful personality, and amazing editing skills, and to my publisher, Matthew Lore, who is one of the most fascinating people I've ever met. I am honored to be a part of Marlowe & Company. Thanks to all the others at Marlowe and Avalon, including Karen Auerbach, who support this book.

Thank you to all of the soulmates who have shared your stories with me. Many of you appear in this book, and you will probably never know how much your stories inspire others to call forth their own love.

Thanks to my dearest friends, whose support I feel and cherish: Judy Waters, Linda Deslauriers, Suzi Lula, Jane Tucker, Renee Piane, Tara Thomas, Barbara Ketchum, Gretchen Vollmer, Marielle Taylor, Melissa Bederman, and so many more. And thanks to my circles of friends who mean so much: my St. Mary's posse from high school who meet annually at Kiawah Island, South Carolina (Buff, Liz, Lisha, Laura, and Michele); The Gang (whom I talk about in the book—Andrew, Dee, Christine, Cat, James, Barbara, Barb, Rob, and Sara); Nuclear Family; my Vanderbilt buddies; and my Agape Practitioner colleagues, including the Goddess Practitioner Group and Mom's Group.

Thank you to P.K. Odle for expert Feng Shui advice and to New Entrepreneurs for their professional networking support.

To my private clients, thank you for enriching my life and trusting me enough to share yourselves with me. You have inspired me in much of this material, and the years we have worked together are precious to me. I fall in love with each one of you. I am grateful for my neighbors on our charmed little block at the beach. I prayed for a friendly place to live, and I got all of you. And thanks, too, to everyone who has been helped by my work: the workshop attendees, the readers, and the customers who have used our products. You inspire me and keep me going.

Notes: While all of the love stories in this book are real, some of the names and minor details have been changed to protect the privacy of those who wish to remain anonymous.

The examples in this book tend to be heterosexual. But I believe everyone has a soulmate regardless of sexual orientation. I work with gay groups as well as straight ones, and the work is no different.

Introduction

A serendipitous incident happened in a support group with which I was involved. The group included single women of all ages. The eldest in the group was sixty-five-year-old Frances. Recently widowed, love was the furthest thing from Frances's mind. One weekend she flew to join friends in another city. The first night, a man showed up unexpectedly at the same friends' house. Arthur, seventy-two, had gotten his weekends confused and came for dinner a week earlier than invited, a happy "coincidence" as it turned out. For when Arthur's eyes met Frances's, she felt "a jolt of electricity," as she describes it, something she had never experienced in her marriage. The feeling was mutual. Their friends saw little of Frances or Arthur that weekend, as the two began a love affair.

When Frances returned from her trip, her story had quite an effect on the group. Because of her age and what she had just gone through with her husband's death, Frances was the last person anyone expected to find romance. She seemed to be the least likely person in the group to find love, and yet she did! The group realized that if Frances could find love, they all could.

After seeing what had happened with Frances, Karen, an overweight fifty-two-year-old who had never been married, felt emboldened. She decided to put a singles ad in the paper. Karen was blunt in the ad, stating concisely who she was and what she wanted. She got thirty replies, which she weeded down to twelve possibilities. Karen had coffee with all twelve men. The last one was Frank, a carpenter. Sparks flew, and Karen and Frank began a passionate romance that ultimately led to marriage.

The rest of the group was wide-eyed at what had happened, first to Frances and then to Karen. The possibility for love that Frances had opened up galvanized every group member. Within two years, all of the group members were happily in love, walking hand in hand with their soulmates.

I teach seminars on love throughout the country, and I enjoy telling this story to my students. Inevitably, one or two people in the group, the people who have labeled themselves *least likely to find love*, get excited. This story gives them back the hope that, yes, they too will find love. As people embrace this possibility, they open the door for romance beyond their wildest dreams. Once they realize that they can have love, it has a magnetic effect, and love is exactly what they get. My intention with this book is to open you up to love, magnetizing your soulmate in the same manner. As you begin to believe that your One is out there and that you are not left out of love, you become open to love that knows no bounds. This has happened to those with whom I work, even to naysayers who protest that my philosophy is "pie in the sky." (Those are the people who usually fall the hardest!)

It is a spiritual principle that *what you believe acts as true.* As you change your beliefs, your experiences also change. If you believe that love is elusive, that you don't deserve love, or that soulmates don't exist, please ask yourself if you really want to live with such negative ideas. My support group discovered that when they surrendered their limitations, they welcomed in love. Now it's your turn.

This book shows you how to not just welcome in your love but to draw him in magnetically. The premise is that you have a soulmate who is living and breathing somewhere on the planet right this minute. In our cynical society, this may seem hopelessly romantic and unrealistic. But I believe that our current culture of fear and pessimism limits us. Breaking out of this prevalent mood isn't always easy, but it *is* worth it. You have a world of love and magic waiting for you.

What I ask you to do is to forget everything you've heard about love, romance, and dating, and start over. The process we will go through releases superstitions and pessimism about love. We're cleaning your mental closet of old, tired beliefs about dating and about yourself. And we will make room for a new way of seeing love, one that will lead you into the arms of your beloved. Ultimately, what happens as you go through this program is that you change your energy and become a *magnet* for love. With each step that I lead you through, you become more of a draw for your One.

Throughout the book, you will find Magnetization Steps and other exercises to lead you out of old ways of being and into an energy that will bring you love. Simply going through this process is enough. No backflips are necessary.

If you would like to experience this book with a group, there is a Ten-Week Soulmate Magnetization Program outlined in appendix 1. You can either read the book first and then participate in a group, or enlist some friends and experience it together as a group. This is a way to build in support for yourself as you open to love. Choose whichever way works best for you. This process is equally effective whether done in a group or as an individual.

For more than a decade in countless workshops I have helped people open themselves to love. This book is based on my tried-and-true principles. I walk you through the same steps I have used to lead thousands of people to love. It works! I have a file folder overflowing with love stories that have resulted from following this method.

Part of the journey is opening up to a new way of looking at love. Another element is debunking all of the prevalent myths about dating and relationships you've bought into that cloud your vision, such as:

> *A woman over forty is more likely to be killed by a terrorist than married.*
>
> *You must kiss a hundred frogs to find your prince.*
>
> *You have to get "out there" to find love. You won't find it sitting at home.*

These stories will keep you fearful about your prospects for romance until you see that they are simply not true.

The final part of finding your soulmate is tackling the inner work you must do to call forth love. It's not difficult. My clients tell me it's the most enjoyable thing they do every day.

The morass of superstition and fear surrounding the issue of love is so thick in our culture that it takes a big jolt to blast through it. This book is that jolt. It blasts through all of the misinformation, the old wives' tales that can make being single an angst-ridden, hellish stage of life.

When I was single I was a victim of this toxic sludge. Scared to death that I would never find love, I was in a constant state of low-level desperation and despair. I was deeply embarrassed to be single, as though it were some plague. Luckily, I was already a licensed spiritual practitioner directing the Crisis Support Team at the Agape Spiritual Center. We dealt with hundreds of people weekly who were experiencing the same dating anxiety as I was. This work helped me to apply spiritual principles to my love life, and the result was wonderful.

While transforming my own single experience, I helped thousands of people overcome the "single blues" and attract love into their lives. It began with the happy results produced through the crisis support work and led to workshops, published articles, and instructional CDs. I have taught through the Learning Annex, spiritual centers, and at conferences such as the Conscious Life Expo and Awakened World as well as in cities throughout the United States, and this work has had an amazing success rate. I have led many support groups while doing this work. Publications as diverse as *Psychology Today, Seventeen,* and the *L.A. Times* have sought my wisdom on matters of the heart. My published CDs, such as *Manifesting Love* and *Releasing a Person,* have sold thousands of copies, and my Web site attracts tens of thousands of visitors each month. My help in attaining love is widely sought after, and now with this book, I happily offer my love life makeover to an even wider audience.

❤ ❤ ❤

Before I began this journey, I thought love was a long shot. All I saw were desperate single people and unhappy marriages. Now I believe in soulmates. Never have I met more couples who clearly belong together. Everywhere I look, I see long-married couples who are still happy. The joy of my life is seeing people blissfully in love and going to countless weddings where those who didn't believe in soulmates are now marrying their own. Yes, the divorce rate may still seem high, but I expect that to change as people begin to open up to the idea of a soulmate and are willing to wait for this love rather than marry for other reasons.

I feel so lucky to have been given this gift of hope and wisdom to share. Now I give this gift to you. You're invited to join me in this happy world of love in which I live. Some cynics may call it a pipe dream, but whatever it is, I choose this world over the old paradigm I used to believe in. Sure, you can believe that love is rare and that your chances are slim to none for finding it. You can paint yourself as a tragic victim who, through the luck of the draw, is relegated to being alone and unhappy. Or you can embrace the message of this book and believe that you get *not* just love, but the *love* of your life.

Oprah Winfrey told the story of how, as a little girl living in poverty, she used to look out her window and wish that she would one day have a few trees of her own to look out upon. At that time she could not have imagined that as a grownup, she would see not just a few trees out her window, but literally *acres* of them . . . all hers. "God can dream a bigger dream than you can," concluded Oprah. So dream as big as you can in terms of love, and let God do the rest. The results will surprise you!

What I have seen in my workshops and in my own life, every day, is that believing in love, walking forward in faith, is the only requirement for attracting your One. This book will help you find that faith and transform you into a magnet for your soulmate. There really is "a lid for every pot," an old Southern expression that I'm fond of repeating. You have just begun the journey of attracting yours. For the majority of people who undergo this program, love comes very quickly. But for some it may take a bit longer as a lifetime of negative thinking is rewired. It may not be as easy for them, but it's worth sticking to the program. The results are priceless.

So buckle up for an exciting ride that ends with a relationship full of crackling chemistry. In case you're wondering what happened to Frances and Arthur, the older couple who met by "coincidence," their story has a happy ending. Frances ended up relocating to Arthur's city and moving in with him. We all missed her but reveled in her tales of trotting the globe with Arthur, walking hand in hand with him through adventures and intimacy. They believe they are soulmates, and they continue to bask in their love.

Now your journey into the arms of your own soulmate begins . . . enjoy every minute of it!

Love Will Find You

1

Crackling Chemistry

The First Magnet: Believe He's Out There

I believe that we are entering the era of the soulmate. Why? Because as we progress as a society, there is no reason for people to pair up and be together other than that they are soulmates. No longer are there any economic imperatives for marriage. Men and women alike can make their own way. No longer is there as much societal pressure to get married. In 2001 the U.S. Census Bureau reported that the number of people who waited later to get married significantly increased between 1970 and 2000, and an increasing number didn't marry at all.[1] In addition, being a single or unwed parent no longer has the stigma it once had. Even not having children is an increasingly acceptable option. Divorce is not only allowable but also common. So the only motivation for being in a relationship is love.

Many studies have shown that uncoerced marriages, unions prompted not through any outside pressure but simply the feelings of the couple, are the ones that last. In 2005 the U.S. Army did a personnel study that concluded that marriages entered into by self-motivation alone were the best ones, the ones that lasted and proved the happiest. The army offers incentives for service personnel to be married. But couples whose marriages were influenced by these incentives were more likely to divorce than those whose only reason for being together was love rather than convenience, economic reason, army incentives, or other concern.

If this next paragraph on soulmates sounds a little far-fetched, simply know that someone out there is meant just for you. And the more you believe that you have a true love, the quicker you will attract that person.

Some schools of thought call your One, the person you were meant to be with, your "twin soul" or "twin flame." More commonly, we know this special someone by the name *soulmate*. This is a person who was created at the same time you were. He or she is your mirror image as a soul (not physically, though some soulmates look like brother and sister or *start* looking alike after they are together for a while). The two of you were separated after your soul birth (not your physical birth here on Earth), because you each had a spiritual journey and a purpose. At the right time you will be reunited and will continue your journey together.

Whatever you believe about the concept of soulmates, I do hope you'll at least consider the notion that there is someone just for you. I believe that it is not possible to miss your soulmate, that forces beyond your control will propel you into each other's arms. Nothing will keep you apart. You can expedite the process of coming together with your One through the process you have already begun with this book.

NON-SOULMATES

While there is only one soulmate, there may be other people you will walk with during part of your journey. A person may not be your soulmate, but your connection may be very deep. Perhaps the two of you have karma to work out together. Perhaps you have some important learning to do together. Perhaps he is preparing you in some vital way for your soulmate. How do you tell the difference between a non-soulmate and your soulmate? When you're with your soulmate, the relationship never ends, and your love never wanes. When you're with someone else, the romance will end, and there's no helping it. If it's not working out, if you're not together, chances are this person is not your soulmate. If he is, he'll come back to you, and the relationship will work out.

> *A true love relationship will never work out with someone who is not your soulmate. It will always work out with someone who is your soulmate.*

This may sound far-fetched, but, to use a common saying, the proof is in the pudding. The Universe does not deny you love and would not hold your soulmate from you. You will unequivocally end up with your One. Practically speaking, this means that if a romance doesn't work out, he couldn't possibly be your soulmate, so don't despair. The end result, being together or having it end, is one of the best ways to measure if someone is your One.

Other signs that he's *not* your soulmate are:

- It's not flowing. The relationship feels like work and seems out of sync somehow.
- You fight a lot.
- You feel incompatible on many levels.
- You can't quell your doubts about him.
- The passion is not there.
- You are not equals in some sense, either in maturity, financially, or in terms of responsibility.
- You have constant anxiety about the relationship. It's not making you happy.
- He does not make you feel stronger, but instead weakens you.
- You don't feel that you can be completely honest with him. He doesn't listen to you and doesn't feel like a friend.
- With him, you feel like you're "settling." Because you don't want to have doubts for the rest of your life, you won't stay with anyone you'd be "settling" for. As discussed later, desperation is not a good basis for decision making.

NOTHING WILL KEEP YOUR SOULMATE FROM YOU

I will repeat this throughout the book. It is not possible for you to miss your soulmate. You may be able to delay her arrival with cynicism or by staying in a dead-end relationship, but ultimately, NOTHING WILL KEEP YOUR SOULMATE FROM YOU.

♥ ♥ ♥

Living Thousands of Miles Apart Will Not Keep Your Soulmate from You: Renee and Joe lived three thousand miles away from each other. Renee had never been married, and she was forty years old. Joe, forty-five, had been married twice and had given up hope that love was in the cards for him. When Renee went back home to Delaware for a family funeral, she met Joe at one of her favorite beach hangouts. They quickly recognized each other as the One they had longed for. Despite the long distance between them, they managed to see each other every other weekend until Joe finally moved to California to be with Renee. They got married in a ceremony that left no eyes dry.

Being Overweight or "Over the Hill" Will Not Keep Your Soulmate from You: It is never too late for love, as evidenced by the story of Frances, sixty-five, and Arthur, seventy-two. Karen, who had always believed that her weight was an obstacle to dating, found her soulmate, Frank, who loves her curves. No matter what you fear your Fatal Flaw is (explained in chapter 2), nothing will keep you and your soulmate apart.

Maya was sixty-nine when she finally learned what it was like to be with her soulmate. At that age she met Ed, seventy-three. Both had been widowed after unhappy marriages. Both describe their union as bringing them happiness they didn't know could exist. Their relationship is easy, companionable, and fun, unlike any love either had known before. Maya says there were good reasons for her marriage and other romances, so she doesn't mind that it took sixty-nine years to unite with Ed. "I'm not looking back. I'm too busy relishing the joy I feel with Ed."

Being Unready Will Not Keep Your Soulmate from You: It is possible that you could set up roadblocks that prevent you from uniting with your soulmate for a while, but if you open yourself to love, love will find you. Anna's friends described her as a "hard" person, emotionally shut down. So many people told Anna that her demeanor kept men away that she started to believe it. She told me that she had a lot of work to do to open up and be ready for her soulmate. I told her that there's no "being ready." You don't have to wait until some magical moment when you have dealt with all of your "baggage" and are perfectly evolved. (Believe me, your growth will continue even after you are with your soulmate.) Anna began believing that maybe she could have love, no matter what her friends said.

Our work to help her discover she had a chance at love paid off. The soft-spoken Vince arrived and fell in love with Anna, hardened exterior and all. His sweetness propelled Vince past all of Anna's emotional walls and right into her heart. Her friends can't believe what's happened to her.

She's become a "softy," "a ball of mush," and "amazingly relaxed," they say, since she and Vince got together. The lesson here is that where the wrong people fail or are put off, your soulmate will find a way through to you.

Other People Will Not Keep Your Soulmate from You: Kate's best friend, Sherry, was a vamp. She exuded sexual energy. Even though Kate was attractive, she felt like a wallflower around Sherry. The reserved Kate watched in despair as countless men she was attracted to played up to Sherry while ignoring Kate. Even a couple of Kate's dates were distracted by Sherry. One day Kate met Richard at a party. Kate was with Sherry. Richard met both women and yet to this day doesn't remember meeting Sherry at the party. He literally could not see past Kate. The two are now married, and Kate explains that, in retrospect, she can see that Sherry served as a screening device for her. The wrong men didn't notice Kate because of Sherry's dazzling energy. But Richard, her soulmate, only had eyes for Kate and never even noticed Sherry. If you think someone is keeping love from you or taking away your spotlight, don't worry about it.

Your Soulmate Will Not Be Able to See Past You.

Divorce Will Not Keep Your Soulmate from You: You've heard stories of couples divorcing only to remarry within a few years (or decades in some cases). In the interim they may even marry someone else. But a divorce won't keep soulmates apart. Neither will another relationship. Even if you break up for a while, if you and another person are soulmates, you'll end up together.

Special Challenges Will Not Keep Your Soulmate from You: I can describe many examples among my clients and workshop attendees who hooked up with their One even though they are physically challenged or battling a difficult illness. If you think you have no chance for love because you use a wheelchair, are HIV positive, or are undergoing chemotherapy, think again. This may be the perfect opening into your heart, allowing the vulnerability that is necessary for love to walk through your door.

LOVE WHEN LEAST EXPECTED

Mary became gravely ill shortly after she began dating Randy. Feeling terrible, unattractive, and despondent, she assumed he would evaporate from her life. What guy could be attracted to a depressed girl who was incapacitated with a chronic condition and flat on her back with matted hair and no makeup? Well, Randy was attracted. Mary's vulnerability while battling her disease made him fall in love with her. Not only did he stick with her through weeks of operations and therapy, but he actually proposed to her while she lay in her hospital bed. His love helped to heal her. Against all odds, Mary began to recover. The two got married, and Mary continued getting better, confounding her doctors. She ultimately did what the medical profession said she could not do and had a child with Randy. They are blissfully happy, and Mary's faith in love and in God has increased manyfold.

HOW TO TELL IF HE'S YOUR SOULMATE

How will you be able to tell if someone is your soulmate? The adage that "you will just know" is not far off. Your gut will tell you, and nothing will keep you apart. You'll be thrown together, propelled together, drawn together until it "takes."

Recognizing your soulmate is fairly easy. Indications that he's the One are:

- You've fought with every boyfriend you've ever had, but you two never fight.
- Everything flows with the two of you. You feel in sync, and it's magical.
- You feel strange, even weird, as the two of you get closer. You're not used to this. Remember: things with your One will be different than they've ever been. Feeling odd is a good sign.
- The two of you fit together like a glove. You are compatible and complement each other well.
- Your relationship is steeped in both romance and friendship. He may even feel like your best friend.
- He strengthens and uplifts you rather than tearing you down or weakening you.
- You feel a deep, even spiritual connection with him.

A COMMON SOULMATE QUESTION

Q. What about people who end up alone, like my Aunt Emma, who is eighty and never got married? Does she have a soulmate? If so, where is he?

A. There are many possibilities as to why your Aunt Emma never married. Here are two of them:

- She may still meet her soulmate even at this late time of life. I've worked with many people who do find their One toward the end of their time on Earth. Inevitably, it's worth the wait. Every experience they've gone through has prepared them for this great love.

- Aunt Emma may not be ready for her soulmate in this lifetime. That may sound strange, except the majority of people do believe that life goes on after we die. It is my belief that some people aren't meant to be with their loves quite yet, but perhaps it will be time for love as they go on with their lives in another place—heaven or another realm or lifetime. People who are not meant to be with their soulmate during their lives on Earth don't have a strong desire for that kind of love. They're content alone and may have trouble settling down.

  I believe that the desires of our heart are put there by God. These desires propel us toward their fulfillment. Some people simply may not long for a soulmate, which means they have another path. For the large majority of us who long for our One, we do unite with our soulmates, and they will be magnetized to us.

The way soulmates grow to recognize each other is as varied as all other aspects of coming together. Some people know right away. Love at first sight does happen, and many people don't delay in plunging in all the way. For example, Drea and Kendall ran off to Vegas and got married after dating only six weeks. Ten years later they are still together and have several children. Tales abound of people who got married quickly and stayed together until their deaths. You often hear: "I knew I would marry her the minute I laid eyes on her" or "I saw him, and I whispered to my best friend, 'That's my future husband.'"

Other soulmates are a slow grow. Which group you fall into can depend on how open you are to romance. If you have erected emotional walls or barriers to love, it may take longer for you to understand that your new love is your soulmate. This is often true of those who have been hurt in romance. Their hearts are well guarded, and they're slow to allow themselves to be vulnerable. People who have been celibate and haven't dated in years also may take longer to open up to their soulmate and recognize their One.

Hattie hadn't dated in two years, so when Tom came along, she was unsure if he was *it* for her. But she found herself more and more drawn to him. He never made a misstep, and while on a date with another man, she was startled to find herself thinking about Tom the whole time. She showed up at his house after the date at 3:00 in the morning, and he happily welcomed her into his arms. Hattie and Tom had a beautiful wedding, and are now walking hand in hand through life with their three children and dog. Hattie no longer has any doubts that Tom is the One for her.

I'LL KNOW HER THE MINUTE I LAY EYES ON HER

I hear this a lot, and I must offer a word of caution. While I mentioned earlier that love at first sight does happen, it is rarer than you might think. Many of us who have been around the dating block once or twice have erected emotional walls. It takes awhile for us to bond to another person, to let them in. *It is far more likely that your relationship with your soulmate will be a slow grow.* In her studies, research sociologist Ayala Pines found that love at first sight occurred only 10 percent of the time. The most popular scenario was falling in love as a gradual process.[2] If you have ever been around someone for a while—at work, at church, or in a group of friends—and suddenly find you have a crush on him, you know what I'm talking about. This is why so many office romances develop. In this sense, I think Europeans are smarter in their dating rituals. They hang out in groups of friends rather than going on one-on-one dates, where there is inherently a lot of pressure on the couple. As the group spends time together, an attraction between two people occasionally occurs. At some point the two will agree to some one-on-one time to explore the attraction they feel for each other. Because studies have shown that most attractions change, it behooves you to give your date a chance. The statistics on the magnetism that one person has for another upon first meeting reveal that the level of attraction *almost always* changes as two people get to know each other. The attraction either diminishes or heightens as the couple spends time together. This is why you need to give your date a chance rather than making a snap judgment that she is wrong for you or that the chemistry is not there.

You may not know yet, and it probably *will* change, one way or another.

TRAIN WRECK LOVE

In my work I often meet couples who have *crazy love*. Crazy love is just what you might imagine, and maybe you've even experienced it. It is a highly dramatic relationship in which emotions run high. It brings up every unhealed wound each partner has, and they push each other's buttons in a big way. This kind of relationship is good for growth and is often depicted in movies and books (think Scarlett and Rhett, Heathcliff and Cathy). It makes for good drama, but in real life your relationship with your soulmate will be much calmer and will run deeper.

If you're in crazy love, you probably have not yet found your soulmate. If you are so attached you cannot imagine giving up the relationship, then take the opportunity to examine what the relationship arouses in you. People who have emotional wounds find it easy to become attached to a person who replicates old familiar patterns of abuse, denigration, or discord. We mistake something we are used to for love. Work on healing your insecurities, dissolving the part of you that loves to argue, is insecure, attracts abuse, or wants to be right all the time. In chapter 10 I go into more detail about just what you can do to transform your crazy love into the soulmate love that is waiting. I also highly recommend the book *Getting the Love You Want*, by Harville Hendrix, as an excellent guide for healing your worst relationship tendencies. If the two of you are growing and willing to work on your differences, there is a slight chance that you can go from crazy love to a soulmate relationship. Every now and then, crazy love grows into mature love. But more often, crazy love is just an unhealthy attachment that keeps you hanging on.

If your crazy love *is* your soulmate, you will know it through the work you do to transcend the drama. As you work together to heal the unhealthy patterns, the relationship will either settle into something solid or fizzle. If he isn't the One, it is a relief to get out of the drama and move toward your soulmate.

Claude and Shelley are crazy love soulmates who got beyond the drama. Shelley got pregnant the first time she slept with Claude, and he did not handle the news well. He claimed the child wasn't his. Shelley had the baby and sued him for child support. Paternity tests proved that he was the father, and he begrudgingly began making payments. He resented the decisions she had made about keeping the baby and suing him for support.

After eighteen months Claude yearned to see their baby. Shelley agreed, for the child's sake. As the two had more and more contact from Claude's visits to their child, the connection they'd had before was evident. They found a healthy way to communicate and gave up their dramatic way of relating. Claude and Shelley grew together in ways they hadn't experienced before. Five years after their first child was born, they married and had three more children. Their relationship has evolved from stormy into the stable, deep love that soulmates share. They have now been happily married for many years.

FITS LIKE LOVE

When you are finally with your soulmate, it is a feeling that takes you beyond any known joy. It is special, an opening into unconditional, full-on love. In the soulmate relationship you probably won't fight (unless you're both from a culture where fighting is a sign of affection and not taken very seriously), even if you've fought with every boyfriend you've ever had.

Ginger longed for the sort of physical affection that had been absent in all of her past relationships. This lack was the greatest source of pain with her last boyfriend, whom she had stuck with for seven years. For short periods he would try to please her by forcing himself to touch her more, but he would lapse back to the distance that came more naturally for him. When they finally broke up, Ginger met Paul and the relationship clicked right away. Paul's problem had been the opposite of Ginger's. Every girlfriend he'd had complained that he touched her too much. When they first began dating, Ginger commented appreciatively about how much Paul touched her. "Is it too much?" Paul asked anxiously, fearing a repeat of the complaints of past girlfriends. "No, it's just right," she smiled. They realized that other people they had dated had been the wrong fit. Paul's affection was what Ginger had been longing for. They suited each other perfectly.

With your soulmate you will feel love to a degree you didn't know possible. Your love will expand your heart so that you'll find love everywhere. Friendships will grow deeper. You'll make up with your family if there has been a rift. You'll have no doubts, no question that he is the right

START A SOULMATE JOURNAL

Before you begin working on the Magnetization Steps described in this book, go out and buy a lined journal. Pay attention to the design of it, and choose one with a cover that reflects love or romance or that in some way reminds you of matters of the heart. At the beginning of this blank journal, write "My Soulmate Journal" plus your name and the date. You will use your Soulmate Journal to do the exercises in this book and track your progress as you open up to love. When your soulmate does come, it's a lot of fun to add the reality of his presence in your journaling to the work you've already done. This is a perfect completion; everyone I've ever worked with gets pleasure from looking back and seeing how similar

one. You'll be too busy being happy with him to worry about concerns that used to bother you. It may feel uncomfortable at first, because you've never had this before. But you'll get used to it. Yes, you *do* get to be this happy. This is what you're heading for, by reading this book and setting your intention to open up to your One.

♥ MAGNETIZATION STEP 1 ♥
DISSOLVE NEGATIVE THOUGHTS AND LET IN HOPE

As the first step in this program of attracting your love, you must begin to eradicate every negative thought you

the person they've been opening to on paper is to the actual person who has appeared.

Journaling is a technique used by psychologists, psychiatrists, coaches, and trainers as a way of expressing our thoughts and feelings, examining our internal mechanisms, and ultimately affecting change. Feel free to use the journal even beyond what is suggested here as various situations and circumstances come up for you. It is a key tool that you will use to begin attracting the love of your life. What you write in your journal is important, so don't hold back. Embrace journaling fully, and you will sense changes happening quickly

have about love. Opening up to love involves ferreting out any limiting beliefs you carry about love, and then releasing these thoughts, ultimately opening up your heart. And there is no place where the inner work is more vital than within your love life. Defeatists share feelings with me like:

> "I just don't want to be disappointed again. Better not to expect too much."
> "I've been hurt badly. I don't believe in love anymore."
> "Dating in this city is impossible."
> "I'm convinced that everyone gets love but me. I'm left out."
> "There are no good men left."

Everyone I work with has some sort of belief that holds them back, something that keeps them from being open to love. If any one of the defeatist remarks above reminds you of your own outlook, vow right this minute to give up that attitude. It is not helpful and will delay you from bringing in your soulmate. Accept the fact that you need an attitude adjustment. Your inner life is vitally important to pulling in your soulmate. Abandon your cynicism now, and instead begin doing the inner work to bring on love. Our ultimate goal is to put you in a frame of mind where you can send out the all-important soul call (described in chapter 2). It is impossible to do this effectively when you are a doubting Thomas.

AN EXERCISE IN BELIEF CLEARING

Begin your Soulmate Journal by writing down your deepest fears and negative thoughts regarding love. Try to list all the cynical remarks you've ever made about dating. Also, list everything that has wounded your heart throughout your love life so far. Be thorough. Leave a few lines of space after each entry.

After you are done, go back to each negative thought, fear, cynical remark, and hurt, and replace it with a hopeful attitude by formulating some positive affirmations to replace each pessimistic belief or hurt:

"My soulmate is on her way to me now."
"I deserve love, and nothing can keep my soulmate away from my side."
"My love life is getting better."
"My past love life in no way has any bearing on my future."

"No matter what I've been through, the outlook for my love life is sunny."

Once you've completed this exercise, copy all of the negative beliefs onto separate small pieces of paper and burn each one. Watch them burn, and feel your old negative patterns of thinking evaporating. Say aloud: "I release all of these negative beliefs and all of my past hurts. This is all behind me now."

Then take your journal with the positive statements, and hold it to your heart. Say out loud: "I now accept each of these beliefs to replace my old negativity." Read each affirmation aloud. When you are finished, place your hand on your writing and say out loud: "My love life is nothing but roses from here on out, and I'm beginning the time of my life starting now."

Congratulations! You have just taken the first step in magnetizing your One!

I affirm that even now you are opening to the idea that you have a soulmate. There is someone out there just for you, and you fit together perfectly. As you accept this idea, you will accelerate the advent of love into your life. It is beginning to happen even now.

2

The Soul Call

The Second Magnet: Invite Love in

A major part of finding your soulmate is sending out a soul call. Because the inner work you do is always much more important than any outer action, every journey starts from within. The soul call is the single most powerful part of the work that I do with my clients. I have watched thousands of people connect with their soulmates after taking my workshops or working with me one-on-one, and I credit this success to the process of sending out a soul call.

Why? Because most of us believe that the emotional and mental work we do within is at least as important as anything we do externally. Think this is airy-fairy hoo-ha? Tell that to the coach who wouldn't dream of sending his team into a game without a prayer and pumping up the team with positive affirmations. The prayer and huddle are all about the inner work, and the most skilled team in the world could not win if they hadn't done the inner work to prepare for the game. Many phenomenal sports figures have written books focusing not on their outer technique but on their inner process as the key to their success.

You need to believe that sending out a soul call is the fast track into the arms of your soulmate. The bonus is that it's fun. Many of my clients send out soul calls regularly to help them stay in a good, positive space until love arrives.

❤ MAGNETIZATION STEP 2 ❤
SEND OUT A SOUL CALL

Take the following steps to send out your highly powerful soul call:

1. Set an intention.

Take out a piece of paper and write down an intention to open up to your soulmate now, an affirmation of love. "I open up to my divine soulmate now. I step into love." The following techniques seem to work best:

- *Write the intention down.* Even if you don't look at it again for months or years, the written intention seems to take on a mysterious power that rearranges your life in order to fulfill it. I ask my clients to write their intention on a piece of paper and either put it somewhere where they see it regularly (like a mirror or home altar) or tuck it away in their Soulmate Journal to pull out later. I suggest you do the same. Find the perfect place for your intention.

- *Say the intention out loud.* After you've written the intention, stand up and say it out loud like you mean business. There also seems to be great power in stating your intention before a group, even a small one. If you are doing this process with friends, take turns reading your intentions to one another. Or take your intention to lunch and read it for your friends to hear.

The simple acts of writing and verbalizing your intention really can catalyze action. Intentions not only seem to propel you to fulfill them but also help by somehow bringing on circumstances beyond what you could have planned to help them along. It's as though you've unleashed magic into your life.

This is only the first step of your soul call, and yet it alone can be quite transformative.

2. Open up inside.

The stories and theories described in this book so far are probably making it easier for you to have more hope. This is a good start. Further, you need to start really *believing* there is someone out there just for you.

In my workshops, I have the luxury of a few hours with the participants to open them to a hopeful outlook on love. You can do this for yourself. What you've read so far in this book should have primed you for the soul call. If necessary, go back and read chapter 1 on soulmates again. Once you've achieved a better outlook on love and opening your heart, you're ready for the next step of the soul call.

3. Welcome him into your heart.

This step involves saying out loud, "Soulmate, I welcome you into my heart, into my life." Do that now, and imagine you are speaking into the soul of someone who is living and breathing on Earth right this minute. This is true—your soulmate is out there right this minute. As you feel yourself connecting with this person inside, send him or her an invitation, a "soul call" to come to you now. Close your eyes, and imagine that you're standing on top of a huge mountain overlooking a spectacular view with your arms stretched wide open. From this open stance, feel your heart sending out love energy, a homing device that travels outward finding its target, your soulmate. Feel the love reach its target and be aware of the corresponding love sent back to you. Now speak to him again. Say, "I invite you to come to me. I am ready to love you."

4. Visualize and feel your soulmate.

To further get in touch with your soulmate, finding out who she is and other aspects about her, you now should undergo a process of discovery. It's very likely that you already know more about this person than you realize. I believe that you were put on this Earth with certain characteristics and tastes that correspond very specifically with those of your soulmate. Some of your own traits that you imagine are negative may actually be attractive to your love. For example, Janice feared she was too boring, too low-key to attract love. When Jack came along, what attracted him to Janice was her calm, mellow presence. In his wedding vows to her he said, "You give me peace. You are my haven in the storm."

Take some time to search through previous relationships and think about what worked and what didn't. This can aid in understanding the characteristics of your soulmate. Here are some questions to answer:

- What attracted you to each person you've loved?
- What physical characteristics were appealing?
- What about his personality was pleasing to you?
- Why did the relationships end?
- What turned you off about past loves?
- What did you find unacceptable in a relationship?
- What did you love about yourself with past romances?
- What did you contribute to your past loves? What did they say was special about you?
- What is the best relationship you've had so far and why? (This is not an invitation to revisit that relationship. Assume something better is on its way.)

From the clues gleaned in this process, you can create a list of characteristics your soulmate will have, along with a list of traits he will appreciate in you, and a description of what your relationship with him will be like. I find that many of my clients had never even asked themselves these questions, which can provide great insight. It is surprising how often the picture that is gained from this process turns out to be accurate. Your soulmate is someone who was created to fit with you perfectly, and this list can help you to get in touch with who he is and what he's like.

A TESTIMONIAL

Dear Kathryn,

Several months ago, I was cleaning up and found a stack of papers I had to go through. Among them was the flyer from your workshop. On the back was a very specific list of the attributes I wished for in the love I wanted to manifest, which I did in your workshop. I had completely forgotten about that list. As I read it, I got chills. Everything on my list was, indeed, within Steve, and more. And believe me, I was REALLY specific, as you suggested, right down to a man with "nice hands."

I wished for some naughty things, too, "a man who's great in bed," and some spiritual things, "a man who's committed to his spiritual growth" and it's ALL there.

A word of warning regarding the list: Don't take this list as the final word on the identity of your love. The list is simply an exploration. You want to remain open, so bless your list and say, "I will have this or something better." Sometimes the Universe throws in factors and circumstances we didn't even think of and knows what will make us happy better than we do.

5. Put out the welcome mat for your soulmate.

A change in the outer life is a sign of change on the inner. So any outer gestures you make to welcome your soulmate are powerful. There are certain steps you can take to welcome

The list is long so I won't share the whole thing. I just wanted you to know you've got one more satisfied customer right here. Feel free to share my story.

And I'm happy to know that the man I was working on releasing at the time I took your workshop has gone on to find someone he's happy with. My experience with him really taught me a lot and truly prepared me for Steve.

Love and gratitude,

Sanyo

Update: Steve and Sanyo now have a beautiful baby girl and are happier than ever.

your One into your life. This is the final stage of sending out a soul call. Below is a list of possible activities you can do to make room for your love. Pick one or two that seem most appropriate for you.

- Buy a card for your husband before you even know who he is. (This is what I did five years before uniting with my soulmate. I kept it on my altar and gave the grayish, curled-at-the-ends card to Jon on the day we were married. The card read, "Forever is not long enough with you." Jon cried.)
- Make space in your life by paring down your work

hours. I've worked with countless workaholics who push love away by being too busy.

- If you're highly independent, make space in your life by letting people do things for you or even asking them to help. Allow people to open the door for you or make you a meal. Learn to ask for help. This will open a door you may have had closed—the one of being interdependent with other people.
- Hang a crystal in a window in the "love corner" (generally southwest) of your home (a Feng Shui tip).
- More Feng Shui tips, courtesy of expert P. K. Odle: If you haven't had a relationship in several years, change the direction of your bed. Also, remove any mirrors from your bedroom.
- Add a nightstand to the side of the bed opposite from where you sleep, and keep it clear.
- Set a place for your love at the table, even though he's not yet here, and talk to him at dinner.
- Clear out a drawer or some space in your closet for his or her things.
- Buy him a gift, such as a robe, that will make him feel at home in your house. Wrap it and keep it to give to him at the right time.

Don't limit yourself to this list. If you know there is something you need to do to make room for love, do it. This gesture is symbolic as much as anything, and by taking this step you're signaling to the Universe that you are primed and ready for love.

DELLA REESE'S SOUL CALL

Della Reese, star of the CBS television show *Touched by an Angel* and also a minister, has been married to her husband, Frank, for almost three decades. She called him forth by doing inner spiritual work, and her process was quite effective. Here's what she did:

- She admitted to God that she had chosen badly in the past and asked God to choose her love for her.
- She stopped looking and asked God to bring her soulmate ***to her*** instead.
- To establish the fact that she had faith, she got rid of her old bed and prepared a new bed for her love, complete with new linens and pillows. She acted like he was already in her life, talking to him and sending him love.

The results were almost immediate, and this couple is a wonderful example of the powerful force within that brings soulmates together.

SOUL CALL SENT!

If you have taken all of the steps outlined in Magnetization Step 2, then consider your soul call sent. You have just magnetized yourself for love, and no doubt you will see the results of this powerful process shortly. Just for fun, revisit any of these steps whenever you feel moved. For example, if you go on a really bad date and recognize another trait or characteristic that you just can't deal with in a mate, add it to your soulmate list as a nonnegotiable item. Or if you find you're slipping into negative thinking about love, repeat your affirmation on a regular basis.

While it may seem easy to say, and almost too easy to believe, your most important task now is simply to remain open and in a positive state. This—the soul call—will help the rest of the steps that follow fall into place.

I affirm that your soul call has been sent and received. You will receive proof of it in the coming days and weeks. Somewhere out there, someone who is living and breathing is traveling toward you, preparing to come into your life.

3

"He'll Run Screaming from the Room"

The Third Magnet: Put Your Fears to Bed

Being single can make you feel vulnerable and bring up every insecurity you may have. Almost every client I've worked with is sure they have a characteristic that makes them unlovable. They've gone to great lengths to hide this imperfection and fear it being exposed. When I asked my client Jody (who insisted her moles were too hideous for any man to love) to name her worst fear about exposing her "flaw," she replied:

"He'll run screaming from the room."

I might've laughed at the ridiculousness of this worry except for the fact that her voice held deep pain. I worked with Jody to deal with the fear, even going so far as asking her to pull up her shirt so that I could see the moles, and suggesting she wear a midriff for a day around the house. It was slow going, but Jody's attitude did improve. The most healing milestone of all was provided by her new love, the man who turned out to be her soulmate.

The moment of truth arrived after Jody and her new boyfriend began spending nights together. One morning, Jody was asleep in his bed, naked, when he came in with coffee for her. Sunlight was streaming through the window when he pulled the sheets back. She shrank away, half expecting him to, yes, *run screaming from the room*. "A constellation!" he exclaimed. He began kissing the field of freckles and moles that dotted her stomach, while she struggled to understand why he didn't recoil in horror. The two are now married, and she has overcome her phobia so well that she lets their young children connect the dots on her tummy with a marker.

I call the "hideous" secret that each person believes might repulse others the Fatal Flaw. For women, it tends to be physical. I had one client who went to great lengths to hide the acne scars that she believed pocked one side of her face. She made sure the "blemished" side was always away from her date's view. Only she could see the scars. I looked for them in broad daylight and could find nothing. For men, the flaw tends to be a career or financial situation. Cam was sure no woman could love him after he declared bankruptcy. He believed that women were attracted only to highly successful guys with major portfolios. It wasn't until their fifth date that he confessed to Emily about his financial problems. She took the information in stride and was touched that he chose to be honest. This heartfelt disclosure was one of the factors that made Emily fall in love with Cam.

A FATAL FLAW DISSOLVED

Hannah was overweight, and as I worked with her she insisted that no man could love her as long as she was carrying so many extra pounds. She felt hideous. Her anxieties were exacerbated by several family members who made unkind comments like, "If you're ever going to get a man, you'll have to lose at least fifty pounds." (No doubt these family members were part of the origin of her mistaken belief that you have to be thin to have love.) Hannah and I continually worked on this issue. Then a miracle occurred. While visiting a friend in a hospice, Hannah met a group of hospice workers who were all borderline obese. They seemed like angels to her in their radiant compassion for the sick. She had never seen more beautiful women, skinny or fat. She realized that the way she saw these women was exactly the way her soulmate would see her. After years of struggle, an overnight change occurred in Hannah. No longer did she believe that her weight would keep love from her. Finally, she was able to see how beautiful she truly is. And love followed shortly.

In reality there is no such thing as a Fatal Flaw. Every single thing about you, even your imperfections, will endear you to your love. These stories about Jody's moles and Cam's bankruptcy illustrate a lovely saying that I believe points to a deep truth:

> *We are admired for our strengths and loved for our weaknesses.*

The idea of the Fatal Flaw is one that evaporates when you're with your soulmate, who can't see past you and is too busy kissing you in that dreaded place for you to worry about it further. Insecurities tend to surface when you're single, and this is a perfect time to face them and heal them. Do you really think something as petty as a haircut, the wrong makeup, a physical flaw, or one little mistake could scare your One away?

REJECT REJECTION

When you see small children playing, you can see that they are absolutely confident. They know they're perfect. If one child makes a critical comment to another, he may get shoved or ignored, but his comment is not taken as a sign that something is deeply wrong with the other child. Within moments, all is forgotten, and the children are happily playing with one another again.

> *There is no such thing as rejection.*

The notion of rejection is one we learn as we grow up.

Society teaches it to us. We are taught how to recognize scorn when we see it, to be deeply hurt, and even to worry that there is something wrong with us at the core. Labels are often given that condemn a child completely. But no one on this planet is simple enough to be reduced to a single word such as "loser," "doormat," "bully," "nerd," "diva," or "wallflower." The handful of people I have met who *don't* fear they have a Fatal Flaw generally grew up with a charmed existence: supportive parents who never questioned their worthiness and a school/neighborhood environment that was loving and egalitarian. As you can imagine, this is rare.

The good news is that you can heal the part of you that has bought into the idea of rejection and feels insecure. It's a matter of changing your perceptions and even reframing your past. When you believe in rejection and are sure there is something deeply wrong with you, you tend to go through life looking for who might hurt you next. Who will reject you? Who will notice your unworthiness? A vital first step in healing this tendency is to start thinking better of yourself. Remember why your friends and past loves have said they love you. Think of what your dog would say about you if he could talk. View yourself through your grandmother's eyes. Pump up your own self-image.

Further, don't let anyone take away your self-image as you build it back up to how it was when you were a small child. This is something you can control. If I came up to you and told you that you had green hair, you would think there was something wrong with me (unless you had just dyed your hair the color of grass). Similarly, if someone tells you that you are a loser—and you know you're not—you would surmise that this person is telling you more about himself (he's judgmental and angry) than about you. But if you secretly fear that, yes, you are a loser, you will be devastated. Do you see the difference? Rejection is your interpretation, not a concrete reality. A secure person who is told he's a loser, will simply assume that the bearer of this news has problems, and if he's a bighearted person will even feel compassion that the person is so deluded.

Instead of taking on any new rejection, quit believing in it. Doing so may be easier said than done, but try the following exercise. With practice, it becomes easier. The next time you experience what you perceive as a slight, examine the situation more deeply. Who slighted you? What does this tell you about her? If a date doesn't call you back, just assume that the Universe is ensuring that you don't waste time with someone who is not your soulmate. Instead of spending hours agonizing over what you did wrong, shrug it off, telling yourself it was a bad fit. Understand that your soulmate, who is out there being drawn to you even now, is incapable of passing you by. Make this your mantra until you truly accept it:

There is no such thing as rejection, only the wrong fit.

As you heal the rejected part of yourself, the world will appear differently to you. No longer will it be scary. You will be better able to see the love that is extended to you from all sides. Fear will no longer control you, and you will find a freedom that you never knew existed before.

DON'T USE THIS CHAPTER . . .

. . . as an excuse to quit caring about how you look. That is not the intention. As the mother of four boys, I can imagine a guy reading about being yourself and deciding he no longer needs to take regular showers. Just because you now know how wonderful you are "as is" doesn't mean you can abandon basic grooming. Every person tries to enhance their appearance, from choosing clothing to putting on makeup to shaving or using cologne. It's where you draw the line that counts. When asked why he omitted flaws when portraying his subjects, Andy Warhol retorted that many features such as pimples, wrinkles, and the like were transitory, and he chose to reproduce the essence of those he illustrated without their imperfections.

I don't judge even those people who get plastic surgery or other treatment to enhance their appearance. What's important is simply the degree of energy you put into improving the way you look. In talking with a reputable plastic surgeon, he commented that a large majority of those who came to him should have been addressing psychological issues of insecurity rather than getting any work done. He sent them to a psychologist before he would schedule a physical procedure. This is why so many people get addicted to plastic surgery. However, it's not their imperfections that are the problem but their self-hatred. They can't erase that through enhancement, which is why changing your attitude about your own perceived flaws is so important.

NO COMPETITION

A freeing fact is that there is no competition in love. If what you thought of as your Fatal Flaw had you comparing

yourself with others and coming up short, you can now let that notion go. It should be easier now that you've begun healing your idea of this flaw and its mythical ability to send dates screaming from the room. In chapter 1 I mentioned that your soulmate will not be able to see past you. I gave the example of Kate and Richard, and how even Kate's vampish friend, who made most guys go *schwing*, didn't register with Richard. He was too smitten with Kate to notice anyone else in the room, even the vamp friend.

Over and over again, I've seen the idea of competition in love shot to pieces. It is a waste of time to try to compete with your vampish friend or suave buddy. Try to think of your supposed competition as your *screener*. They help you sift through potential mates. And while at times you may feel like the unpopular wallflower, it only takes the magical One to change all of that. Any given moment when you feel like you're somehow losing in the game of love is just a brief snapshot of your life. It is not the sum total of it, and situations shift quickly. I've been to many weddings where the "wallflower" friend is at the altar while the femme fatale friend is still single, scoping out eligible wedding-goers.

Here is the simple truth:

Your soulmate can't see past you.

You are "it" for him or her, and no one else will do. The concept of competition, one-upping one another in dating, snaking someone else's love, does not hold up under scrutiny. The idea of jockeying for love has nothing to do with love itself. Instead that notion proves to be irrelevant

and therefore not worthy of attention. Love is not logical in this way. If you find yourself falling into feeling competitive or at a disadvantage, remind yourself that you're needlessly torturing yourself. If anything, competition, one-upmanship, rivalry, and viciousness can get in the way of love rather than increase anyone's chances of finding it.

♥ MAGNETIZATION STEP 3 ♥
HEAL YOUR FATAL FLAW BELIEF

Search your heart for your insecurities, and release these hidden fears of being undesirable.

- In your journal, make a list of the characteristics that you're scared make you unlovable. They are traits that you hide, are squeamish about admitting, or try to change in yourself. Often they are also what you judge harshly in others.
- Highlight one or two items on the list that trouble you the most.
- Take a moment to ponder the notion that you have no idea what anyone else, especially your love, will think about this Fatal Flaw. Therefore, you are the one who is judging yourself before you even get out of the gate. Refuse any further rejection of any sort internally right now, and vow to continue denying it in the future.
- Think about past loves for whom this characteristic was no big deal. They loved you anyway. In your

Soulmate Journal write down names of people who overlooked your Fatal Flaw.

- If you can't think of anyone who was okay with your Fatal Flaw, then realize that we often attract those who mirror our own self-judgments. Vow to never let anyone in again who sees you as less than amazing. Working on healing your own self-judgment is a wonderful first step in this direction.
- Accept, even try to love, your Fatal Flaw as being part of your own, imperfect, lovable self. If this is difficult for you, think of some of the flaws in past lovers and how accepting you were of them. Learn to be just that accepting of your own weaknesses. This isn't always easy and can take some work. But any difficulty you have in taking this step is well worth it. You can then be free to live life unfettered by what can be a crippling fear of having this flaw unveiled. Write down under the highlighted Fatal Flaws you listed the reasons why they don't make you hideous or unlovable.
- Say out loud, "I forgive myself for judging myself as unlovable, fat, old, and so on."
- Close your eyes and visualize your One discovering your flaw and not only loving you anyway, but thinking it's endearing. (Happily, I have heard this story played out more times than I can count.) Describe this revelation in your Soulmate Journal.
- Say out loud: "There is no competition." Now think of someone you feel threatened by, someone you

feel always gets the girl or whose light you fear shines brighter than your own. Bless that person silently and write in your journal: "I bless [*person's name*] for getting his [or her] love." Now say the following: "We both get love, and my love can't see past me." Write this down next to your blessing for the other person.

Note: If someone you meet actually does run screaming from the room or the equivalent of it, thank God for weeding out the wrong one for you more quickly. Don't take it personally. Remember this: *there is no such thing as rejection, only the wrong fit.* Your One will be drawn to your vulnerability.

THE SECRET APHRODISIAC

As you put your Fatal Flaw to rest and quit believing in competition, something magical will happen. You will begin to exude more confidence. And as we explore in the next chapter, there is no more powerful aphrodisiac than confidence, a nice bonus for undergoing the process of healing your insecurities.

Another bonus is that accepting your Fatal Flaw can allow you to finally abandon any urge toward manipulation once and for all. Manipulation often finds its way into dating and love situations. Why? The parties are scared that they do not deserve to have love without playing a game or stacking the deck in their own favor by such acts as stringing along several people, pumping up their image with bragging or in another way manipulating the situation. Once you understand that you deserve love as you are, you no longer feel as if you have to do backflips, make yourself look better in someone else's eyes, or do a dog-and-pony show to attract love. Dating becomes much simpler.

I affirm that the last vestiges of your belief in your Fatal Flaw are now dissolving. You see how beautiful and wonderful you are. You accept your innate lovability. You are precious, and increasingly you are able to understand this.

4

How Will She Know You if You're Not You?

The Fourth Magnet: Shine Your Unique Light

"Be yourself" is a dictate that every dating coach on the planet espouses, but what does it mean? Why would anyone need to *say* this? It is because in order to cover up our vulnerabilities or perceived flaws, too many of us have tried to be something we're not, contorting ourselves to fit into a supposed mold of desirability. Or we censor ourselves, fearing that if we make just one false move, we'll blow any possibility we may have had for love. The problem with this philosophy is that it just doesn't work. Boning up on your grooming, working out to be at your best—all of these steps toward self-improvement are fine, but that's not what I'm talking about.

Evie had a horrible case of psoriasis. Covered from head to toe with this skin inflammation, she believed she looked repulsive. An attractive redhead, she was not used to feeling disfigured. In the midst of this ailment, she had to take a trip. She wore sweats and no makeup on the plane, figuring that she already looked so bad, there was no sense in dolling herself up.

Upon boarding the plane, Evie was horrified to find herself seated next to a handsome man. Normally, she would have flirted with him, but there was no point in doing that on this flight, looking the way she did. Brad, her handsome seatmate, engaged her in conversation. She figured she had no chance with him, so she found herself being brutally honest with him about herself and her opinions. She held nothing back, and they talked for the entire five-hour flight. Evie had never been so *herself* with a man she found gorgeous, but circumstances were different this time. It was out of the question that he would become a love interest. Wrong! Brad was captivated by Evie's genuineness, and they began dating, much to Evie's surprise. In fact, it had never gone better with a date, and Evie discovered in a most unusual way how sexy being herself could be, psoriasis and all.

THE LINK BETWEEN BEING YOURSELF AND SELF-ESTEEM

The degree to which you are able to be yourself is related to your level of self-esteem. The more you accept yourself and feel good about who you are, the easier it is to behave naturally, as yourself. Signs of healthy self-esteem are:

- not feeling like you're constantly apologizing
- being able to say no without guilt
- experiencing minimal jealousy or envy
- not having money woes
- being able to receive as well as give
- being able to freely admit fault and say you're sorry
- valuing your own intuition and opinions as highly as anyone else's
- not needing to seek approval from others
- when seeming rejection happens, shrugging your shoulders, thinking the other person is missing out, and then getting on with life
- having supportive friends

THE INSECURITY QUIZ

This quiz will help you pinpoint how your insecurity manifests. Read the statements below, and check all that apply to you. Don't worry if you're ticking off many items. I and many people with whom I've worked had a majority of these issues until we healed our self-esteem wounds.

__ I have money problems.
__ I am very jealous when in a relationship. I feel threatened quite a bit.
__ I am envious of others sometimes.
__ I sometimes feel like nothing, completely unimportant.
__ If people aren't noticing me, I feel uncomfortable.
__ I have to act just right and be perfect to feel okay.
__ I'm shy and not empowered to speak up for myself.
__ I am sometimes a doormat.

__ I have been abused either emotionally or physically.
__ I'm codependent and have a hard time saying no.
__ I have difficulty speaking in front of a group.
__ I often worry about what people think about me.
__ I always think I've done something wrong.
__ I'm great at blaming myself. I'm my harshest critic.
__ I can't stand to hear my own voice or see myself on video.
__ Looking in the mirror is painful for me.
__ I don't feel good unless I'm making myself useful.
__ I feel incompetent and/or clumsy.
__ I exaggerate the truth or tell white lies to build myself up.
__ I find myself dropping names or using material things to make myself look better in the eyes of others.
__ I have deliberately tried to make my partner jealous or played games to make sure he or she loves me.
__ When I go to a fancy restaurant or ritzy shop, I feel like a fish out of water, unentitled.
__ I feel like I'm always trying to prove myself.
__ I can instantaneously tell you a list of everything that is wrong with me and why I'll never make it.
__ I'm embarrassed to dance in front of others.
__ I gossip and speak ill of others to feel better about myself.

If you checked more than four of these boxes, you probably have self-esteem issues that need to be addressed. Confronting these issues head-on is the only way you'll learn to be comfortable being yourself. Having insecurities is not your fault, so don't blame yourself for how you feel. Somewhere in your life, in school or in your family, someone told you that somehow you weren't enough. You bought into that. Now is the time to get rid of that idea and understand what a precious child of God you really are.

Growing up, many of us were introduced to an ideal. I have countless clients whose parents held them up to someone else, an older sibling or schoolmate, and found them lacking. The lauded sibling or friend became the ideal that they had to try to live up to. These people internalized the idea that they are somehow lacking, and since then have been trying to heal that misperception. We humans can use the ideal to create dissatisfaction with ourselves and our lives. The problem with an ideal is that it makes no room for us to be who we are, to express who we are without reference to any outside force. A large step toward healing insecurities is to drop the ideal. Whatever or whomever it is, I'm sure they're perfectly lovely. But *they are not you.*

I believe that we are given our unique characteristics, traits, and behaviors because they somehow serve us. The very aspect that may have branded you as not fitting in may become your biggest strength in the end. What I know is that your mate will love the things that make you unique, and they will be what makes you perfect for him.

One of my clients experienced a healing when he traveled home for his twentieth high school reunion. Gray, a frail boy, had been on the fringe of popularity, and his parents constantly pressured him to live up to his popular neighbor, Sam, who had been both quarterback of the school's football team and homecoming king. Gray moved far away, no doubt to get away from the pressure, and hadn't been home since. He had become a successful Internet entrepreneur, finding that his "inner nerd," a part of himself he had always hated, enabled him to make buckets of money and find career fulfillment. In the process of finding his calling, Gray was able to realize what a valuable human being he was. At his high school reunion, he looked good and felt great. There was Sam, still quite social. Feeling good about himself, Gray could see that Sam was not larger than life, but simply another human being. Gray had a good time and realized that he didn't care that much about what anyone thought of him, because he thought he was pretty wonderful himself. No longer did he judge himself as lacking compared to Sam or anyone else. He came away with his ghosts from high school, and any lingering comparison to an ideal that never existed, put to rest once and for all.

SO WHAT DOES SELF-LOVE LOOK LIKE ANYWAY?

One of my early mentors was a doctor named Jill Ruesch-Lane. Until I met her I never had a picture of what a self-loving, confident woman looked like. Jill conducts herself in a confident manner, never questioning herself. She feels secure enough to be able to apologize or admit her mistakes. She has no problem telling you if she thinks something is unfair. Neither egotistical nor self-centered (these aren't signs of good self-esteem), Jill treats everyone she meets with the same regard she has for herself. She exhibits compassion and understanding for others and is a good listener. She thinks highly enough of herself to charge what she's worth, to fight for herself in a very civilized manner if called for, and to draw boundaries if she believes she's being taken advantage of. She is honest, forthright, and is highly regarded in a wide variety of communities, probably because she regards herself highly first.

Many women somehow get an extra dose of insecurity in growing up, which perhaps is not so surprising in a patriarchal society. What patriarchy means to us is that boys and men—and their endeavors—tend to be more highly valued. Hence, we have yet to have a female president; traditionally male jobs are paid better than traditionally female ones like teaching, nursing, and clerical work; and activities and concerns that are feminine are belittled as trivial. No wonder so many women have self-esteem problems. So it has been rare for me to meet someone like Jill, who is a model of confidence. I'm very grateful to know her, because by example she helped me to heal many of my own self-worth issues. Understand that if you are a woman who has security issues, you are in good company and the deck may have been stacked against you via the pervasiveness of patriarchy in our society. Working to better your self-image sets you up to attract your soulmate and obtain the healthy egalitarian relationship that eludes anyone who has not dealt with their lack of self regard.

Another early example I saw of self-love came from a very difference source. One of my clients, Bill, was a computer whiz who worked out of his basement. Everywhere you looked there were piles of papers, open computers, and computer parts all over the floor, plus mountains of debris. The place literally *smelled.* Bill's appearance reflected his surroundings. He wore jeans that were so baggy that they threatened to fall off at any moment, stained T-shirts, and his hair was a messy mop. His glasses were always crooked, and his grooming was lacking. But the way Bill behaved, you would have thought he was the CEO of a Fortune 500 corporation. With such a disheveled home and physical appearance, I would have been embarrassed to even let the UPS man in, but Bill cntertained clients and held meetings in this pigsty. He never offered apologies for his physical appearance or the home office. He would shove some papers off a chair, invite his guest to sit, and conduct meetings in a self-assured manner.

I was appalled but admiring of his confidence. Bill knew he was going places. And indeed he did. Within a year of the time he started his business, he had a large office full of employees, including someone to keep things tidy. He also married a wonderful woman with whom he created a family.

So what does self-love look like? Here are some characteristics:

- You've got good boundaries. No doormat, you're willing to draw the line if someone tries to take advantage of you or if you feel unhappy with how you're being treated.
- You regard yourself highly, knowing you are worthy and inherently important, without being egotistical or dismissive of others.
- You trust that you are deserving of good things in life, and you don't settle for less than what you want or deserve.

- You feel no need to try to be something you're not.
- You don't let so-called rejection make you feel undesirable, because you understand that some people are just the wrong fit.
- You don't let toxic people into your life. You create some distance between yourself and anyone who might cut you down or denigrate you.
- You're not defensive. You know that if you make a mistake, it doesn't negate your worth as a person. Instead, you're able to graciously apologize, realizing that like everyone else, you're human and will make mistakes, even stupid ones.
- You are able to forgive yourself for not being perfect and don't continually blame yourself for everything that goes wrong.
- You don't engage in negative self-talk, denigrating yourself mentally or in front of others.

I invite you to look for examples of people you meet who are self-confident. Observe how they behave. Model their self-loving conduct. Don't try to *be* them, as you must be yourself, but use their example of confidence to change. As any parent knows, modeling, using examples that we see, is the best way to learn a new way of being. Later in this chapter there are some exercises I recommend for addressing any self-love issues you may have. If this chapter seems to hit home for you, please take the time to do these exercises. Self-worth problems are one of the biggest blocks I have seen to attracting true love, not to mention the problems they create in almost every area of your life.

WHY YOU MUST BE YOURSELF TO ATTRACT YOUR LOVE

With regard to love, why is it so important to be yourself and to be confident enough to do so? Your soulmate won't recognize you if you're busy trying to be someone else. It is imperative that you be yourself, eschewing any cookie-cutter model of attractiveness, either on the inside or the outside. The components of attraction are so specific to an individual that there is no way you can make yourself a magnet for everyone. There is no random mold of desirability to fit into. Studies have shown that there are thousands of factors that contribute to attraction, none of which are predictable (other than confidence). The only love you want is your soulmate.

Lisa had buckteeth and was about to get them capped when Alex, the man she was seriously dating, realized that every woman he'd dated had buckteeth. He believed her teeth were one attraction that led him to her and (successfully) begged her not to get the caps.

Ace, a natural introvert, feared that his quiet nature wasn't dynamic enough to attract anyone. He saw loud, aggressive guys frequently "getting the girl," but just didn't have it in him to behave in such an extroverted fashion. Then Ace met Carol at a party. She rebuffed several men vying for her attention to focus on Ace, whose calm demeanor she found charming. They quickly became a couple, and Ace realized that his tranquil nature could be an asset.

Your soulmate will think your seemingly odd traits are attractive. Exuding the confidence that you're good enough exactly as you are is the most powerful magnet there is. Again, keep in mind that confidence has been shown to be a major factor in attraction.

LOVING THE "UNLOVABLE"

Grace hated hairy chests. "Eww!" was what came to mind when she was faced with furry pecs. Then she met Austin on a skiing trip. He wore turtlenecks the entire time, so she didn't realize that he had an extremely hairy chest until they were quite involved. By the time I saw her, she was head over heels in love with him. "I can't believe it!" she exclaimed to me. "I love every hair on his body. I still don't love hairy chests in general, but I love his because it's his." Austin had worried about how hairy he was and had even considered waxing. Grace's acceptance of him "as is" was healing for him and a revelation for her. This is how love works, and you should keep this in mind when thinking of your supposed flaws. Your One loves you for you, and loves everything about you *because it's you.*

Start working on being comfortable in your own skin right now. Dig up any voices inside of you that say you're not enough. How do you believe you are lacking? What do you think a prospective partner might find fault with in you? Every child comes out of the womb whole, perfect, and complete. We stay that way, but most of us get messages along the way that say something about us is not okay. If you have somehow internalized the message that you are flawed, it is time for you to reclaim your self-esteem.

Earlier, when we were sending a soul call (see chapter 2), you did an exercise in which you had to think of why your soulmate will love you. You recalled what former loves enjoyed about you, and even thought of what your dog might say about you if he could talk. It is time for you to start realizing that you are lovable just the way you are. People express feelings to me like:

> "I'm really working on myself, and I'm hoping soon I'll be at the right place to attract love."
>
> "I am so messed up, I couldn't possibly be ready for love. Maybe after a few more years of therapy."
>
> "I'm on a diet, and if I can just lose twenty pounds, then I'll be ready for love."
>
> "Let me get that facelift and some new clothes, then I might think of dating."
>
> "Who could love me? I have no career, old eggs, and no money."

These laments reflect people who think they can't have love until they're somehow perfect or at least *more* perfect. These people are judging themselves as unworthy of love, or even as human beings, because of a particular circumstance. If you find yourself doing this, it is time to accept a simple truth: you don't have to change a thing about yourself to have love *right this minute*. Do you really think that a particular circumstance or quality makes you unlovable? If you walk out the door right now, you will run into at least twenty people who are part of a couple who possess the exact same quality you think makes you unattractive. Love found them and it will find you. I've said it before but it bears repeating, because many of the people I work with need to hear this over and over again until they finally get it:

> There is nothing about you that will repel your soulmate. He will love you unconditionally and will even find your quirks "cute."

It is time for you to become happy now, both with yourself and with your life. Start seeing yourself as through the eyes of God. One of my favorite books I recommend to singles is *God on a Harley,* by Joan Brady. God is insulted because the protagonist fails to see the beauty He gave her when He created her. When she finally loosens up and sees how glorious she is, her soulmate comes along. Start seeing your inherent beauty.

THE MIRROR EXERCISE

At least once every day, look at yourself in the mirror for a few minutes. Take note of what you tend to focus on when you see yourself. Do you notice first what you don't like about your appearance? Perceived flaws? Are there parts of yourself or your face that you avoid looking at? What are your thoughts about how you look? Are they negative? Do you feel differently about yourself when you're wearing makeup and/or are dressed up than you do when you first awaken in the morning or are not made up?

Smile at yourself. Make an effort to focus on what you like about your appearance. Look at yourself and imagine how others see you. Peer deeply into your eyes and tell yourself, "You're beautiful." Think of at least three compliments you can give yourself and say them out loud. At first, this may feel excruciating, but that will improve until you are finally able to accept who you are and see the beauty that you radiate

AN ATTITUDE ADJUSTMENT

Do you silently beat yourself up on a regular basis? Or do you call yourself "stupid" either aloud or in your head when you do something that you deem imperfect? If so, it's time to change. I wish it were as easy as the "attitude adjustments" I give to my children when they're being difficult to deal with. I rub their head with my fingers, make a funny noise, and the moment passes. We laugh, and the tension is dispelled.

Unfortunately, your transformation may take more time. Somewhere along the way you internalized an attitude about yourself that was not admiring. Someone told you that you were stupid or unworthy, and eventually you didn't need their voice to continue that dialogue. You internalized it, and now you do the job of self-denigration with no outside help. This took time, so it can take time to dissolve the voice and change your self-regard.

Begin by catching yourself whenever you start to beat yourself up. From the moment you notice your mind starting in with negative thoughts about yourself, interrupt those thoughts. Without interruption you can sometimes get into what I call a *negative trance*, a self-induced funk that feeds upon itself so that you look up thirty minutes later and discover you've been beating yourself up the entire time. It is important to stop this course of thinking once you become aware of it. The more you practice, the better you'll become at catching yourself before you get into a full-blown self-hatred session.

Once you notice you're going off on yourself, stop the momentum. Awareness is a powerful healer, and just *noticing* that you're going back to this pattern is a remedy to it. After ceasing the negative self-talk, substitute a more reasonable voice. Remind yourself of the following:

- I was doing the best I could.
- Everyone makes mistakes.

- Just because I did something imperfect doesn't mean I am worthless.
- There is nothing wrong with me. I am whole, perfect, and complete in my humanity.
- I am precious and infinitely lovable.

If there are specific areas in which you feel you are lacking, write an affirmation for them, such as:

- *Your Thinking:* I'm ugly.
- *Affirmation:* I am beautiful in the eyes of Spirit.

- *Your Thinking:* I am dumb. I'm stupid. Why didn't I understand that?
- *Affirmation:* I am intelligent. I'm wise and sharp. I'm not the only person who didn't understand it.

- *Your Thinking:* Why couldn't I think of a witty response to that comment? I'm slow.
- *Affirmation:* I am quick, smart, and a good listener.

- *Your Thinking:* Why couldn't I be the one to catch his attention? It's never me who gets noticed.
- *Affirmation:* I will be noticed by the right person, my soulmate. He can't see past me.

BEING YOURSELF WHILE DATING

As I said earlier, dating is not an essential activity for attracting your soulmate (though you will have to at least date her to get to know her). However, for those of you who

INSECURITY AND AFFIRMATION EXERCISE

1. Take some time to think of any aspects of yourself that you believe are weak, where you think you're not good enough. Write down these thoughts in your Soulmate Journal.
2. Now write down *how* you believe you are lacking in these areas.
3. For each of these issues, write a positive affirmation in the present tense that addresses the issue and supports your worthiness.
4. Memorize these affirmations.
5. Get in the habit of saying your affirmations every time one of your issues comes up and you find yourself feeling lacking or beating yourself up. Begin now by stating the affirmations out loud three times, each time with increasing volume and authority in your voice.

choose to take advantage of the vast dating pool available online, a question I often hear is: "How honest should I be with online dating?" My response: "Very honest." Life would be so much easier for online daters if they would just be honest. Dishonesty simply doesn't work. If you use a photo that's twenty years old in your profile, your date *will* notice, believe me. And it will introduce a trace of doubt about your character. In this day of digital cameras and instant photos, there is no excuse for an outdated photo. I guess the mentality goes, "Let me just attract some people with a perfect photo and profile, and then once they *meet* me, they'll see how great I am, even if I'm not just like that."

It doesn't work that way, and from what I've seen the people who have the greatest success in online dating (defined by me as resulting in marriage or a serious relationship) are those who are courageous enough to be themselves. While this doesn't mean laying all of your problems on the table right away (this is self-indulgent and focused too much on the negative), it looks like this:

- Posting a recent, accurate photo that is not airbrushed
- Presenting who you are and what is important to you without having to pump yourself up or exaggerate your skills, hobbies, and so forth
- Clearly expressing what you want

A friend of mine who has had tremendous success with online dating says she advises putting up a lengthy profile so that you weed out people who immediately won't be right for you. Online dating can give a false impression of singles abundance, but since you only want one, the right one, resist the temptation to include anything that will get you five hundred responses. Wading through them will be daunting, and while at first you may feel popular, this overload can thwart your goal to find the One in an easy way.

During a first or second date, it's not appropriate to be painfully honest. But *do* begin a new relationship by not putting on a false persona. Honestly enjoy your date for who and what he is, and express who you are in a clear way.

This means not lying or even fudging answers to any questions. The mentality on this is threefold:

- You need to be yourself so that your soulmate will recognize you.
- You want to set an honest tone for your future relationship.
- Most important, by being yourself you affirm that you are good enough exactly as you are.

Lisa had been looking for love for years without success. She had what she thought was a perfect way of attracting men, with a specific way to dress, to flirt, and to behave. She knew what she would disclose and what was unmentionable. She joined a protest with her union and volunteered to organize part of it. Lisa was paired with a stocky guy to do the work. They both were wearing hats, jeans, and sneakers, and Lisa was not in dating mode, nor did she consider the man, Shep, a potential mate.

Lisa and Shep got to know each other as they worked side by side. Preoccupied with the protest, she was more herself than she usually allowed herself to be. Shep fell in love with her in the course of their project, and she was surprised to find herself reciprocating the feelings. When she realized how crazy she was about Shep, she looked back in horror at everything she had told him. She had poured out her deepest feelings with no censorship. She was afraid she had revealed too much. But then she saw that it was *because* of her honesty, her lack of self-censorship, that he fell for her. It was healing for Lisa to discover that she didn't need any of her dating rules, her guard firmly in place, to find love. Quite the opposite was true: all she needed was to be herself.

The more you question yourself, the more others will, too. The more you get rooted in who you are and even begin to love your own identity, the more the world will open up to you in a surprising way, as Lisa discovered.

Chapter 8, "The Mating Dance," goes into more detail about dating in a different way using these principles. But for now, even before you date, try to practice being more of who you are. For some of us, this is quite a journey. Perhaps no one ever asked you what you wanted or what your style is. Perhaps you've been so busy trying to be okay that you have no idea what you'd really be like if you quit acting in order to please other people. Now is the time to start finding out. The ideal scenario in relationships, and one I see most often in soulmate relationships, is when you are 100 percent yourself and feel more comfortable in your skin than you've ever felt before. Your soulmate's love may help propel you into being more of your genuine self, but now is the time to start learning who you are and begin accepting and loving yourself completely.

MANIPULATION IS NOT NECESSARY

Manipulation can take some of the following forms (some of these have been noted earlier but bear repeating):

- Playing hard-to-get when you really like the person
- Dropping names or pumping yourself up to a prospective love interest

- Pretending to like something you don't to impress your date
- Exaggerating in an online dating profile
- Posting a photo of yourself that is airbrushed or twenty years old
- Hiding information about yourself, even when you've been involved for a while
- Dressing like your boyfriend so that he'll feel more bonded with you—which creates problems because it negates the importance of your own identity and needs

These are a few of the ways we reveal our secret fears that we're not enough. If we thought we were lovable unconditionally, we wouldn't feel the need to be dishonest. We want to find someone who loves us as we are; therefore, manipulation is not a good idea. Beyond that, the subconscious message that we're sending—and that is received even as we try to hide it—is that there is something wrong with us and we must keep it secret. The irony is that the more you accept yourself and choose honesty, the more attractive you become. You exude that most irresistible of qualities: confidence.

THE INDEPENDENCE TRAP

Certain people I work with, usually those who are quite successful in their careers and overly independent, have a difficult time allowing love into their lives. While degrees of independence vary from person to person, I find that overly independent people are actually wounded. They have been emotionally damaged and have decided it's easier not to rely on anyone. In psychological terms, this method of self-protection is called *withdrawal*. Love comes in through vulnerability, but in these people it's difficult to identify such weakness. They've plugged up their vulnerabilities in order to defend themselves from hurt.

People who are too independent have no room in their lives for love. If you believe you don't need anyone for anything, perhaps this is you. Everyone needs to feel wanted, and if you are too self-sufficient, there is no opening for a love prospect to come into your life. So if you have been career-focused without admitting that you have personal needs, think again. Every one of us is interdependent, with personal needs for love, contact, and connection. Denying this with extreme independence is just a cover.

If you are someone who is so efficient that you've engineered your life to avoid needing anyone, your task is to loosen up and let people in. Allow dates to give to you, and allow yourself to receive graciously. Get into the practice of asking for help rather than doing everything yourself. It's much less exhausting and will connect you better to others. I find that when I work with these independent people, they quickly find love just by offering the slightest opening to their hearts.

VULNERABILITY IS STRENGTH

It would seem that people who allow themselves to be vulnerable are weak, but in fact they are the strong ones. People who have gone to great lengths to appear invincible are scared that if they let their guard down, they'll be crushed. But a person who believes he is safe enough to be vulnerable is the *real* strong one. Invulnerability simply doesn't work in love or in any human relationships. Remind yourself of this fact when you are tempted to batten down your emotional hatches. Examples of how you might exhibit vulnerability are: admitting to someone when you are hurt, asking for help when you are overwhelmed, sharing your feelings with a friend or date, even if you're worried they might be perceived as a weakness.

♥ MAGNETIZATION STEP 4 ♥
FIND OUT WHO YOU ARE

Here are some ways that you can discover who you truly are and what you stand for.

1. For many of us, no one has ever asked: "What do *you* want?" "What will make *you* happy?" And we've never asked ourselves this question, either. Think about what makes you happy. What feels good? And what don't you like? Understand that nothing is too trivial to be frowned upon, and you need make no excuses for what you do and don't like. In your Soulmate Journal, make a list of your interests and preferences.
2. Explore the ways you think about yourself. Write down the answers to the following questions and anything that led you to your answer.

- What do I think of my appearance?
- What is my personality like: outgoing, quiet, funny, or serious?
- What do I do well? What do I wish I could do?
- Do I enjoy learning? What book did I last read?
- When do I feel sexy?
- Do I play by the rules or do I stretch them?
- How well do I relate to others? Am I a good listener? Am I a good storyteller?
- Do I feel comfortable with others quickly, or does it take time for me to warm up to them?

3. Start accepting yourself. Remember that however you answered the above questions, there are many people with similar answers who are successful, have amazing love, and enjoy fulfilled lives. Now that you've set this process in motion, you will find yourself noticing more and more about who you are and what you like. Release any judgments as they come up. You can do this in the following way:

- Notice how you are judging yourself, and write the answer down in your Soulmate Journal.
- Ask yourself where this voice of judgment originally came from, and write down your answer in your journal. Most of our self-judgments were internalized at an early age from a parent, friend, or teacher who judged us first.
- Forgive yourself for this judgment. When you were young, you had no way of defending yourself from

it, and it was internalized without awareness on your part. Say out loud: "I forgive myself for judging myself negatively."

- Give yourself some understanding about whatever it is you are judging. It doesn't make you a bad person, and while you can do your best to change it, allow yourself to be imperfect, human like us all. The bottom line is that you are still a worthy being, flaws and all. Take a moment to put your arms around yourself, give yourself a hug, and say aloud: "I am worthy, imperfections and all."

This process is not only wonderful spiritual growth, but it also serves as a powerful attraction force for your love. Feel your love magnetization getting stronger and stronger.

Even now you are becoming more of who you really are. I bless you for realizing that all you need to be is you, understanding that you are enough, as is. I affirm for you more confidence and self-assurance than you've ever had. I release for you any insecurities you've had. Walk forward in faith that you are perfect, whole, and complete.

5

Declutter Your Heart

The Fifth Magnet: Release Old Loves

There is an all-too-human tendency to hang on to past loves. It is easier to picture someone you already know, a person you have been close to, than to imagine a faceless, nameless somebody you have yet to meet. Fortunately in terms of what we can hope for in love, we are not limited to the past, to the way it's always been, or to people we already know.

Almost everyone who attends my workshops is holding on to a past love or crush, either consciously or subconsciously. It is important to clear our energy from anyone we are holding on to. Attachment is common, particularly for those who have gone through a painful breakup or divorce.

WHY WE SPEND TIME WITH MR. OR MRS. WRONG

There are many reasons why people date or even marry the wrong person. Below are some common reasons why people end up together, even though they're clearly not soulmates. I don't believe there are any mistakes in life, so even if one of these explanations doesn't ring true for you, trust that at the time there was a deeper reason why the two of you came together.

1. *You had karma together that you had to work out.* "Karma" is everywhere these days—from perfume scents to TV shows. Even my oldest teen knows what karma is. If you meet someone with whom you have a deep connection, feeling as if you've known him before even though you haven't, the connection doesn't necessarily mean you're soulmates, but it could mean you have some knowledge or talents to teach each other in life. Teachers come in many different forms, including people who push our buttons (therefore exposing the button so that we can get rid of it and become less reactive).
2. *He helped you heal.* Perhaps this person showed you just how ugly anger could be and therefore aided you in dealing with your own anger once and for all. Or perhaps she was the first person to ever show you unconditional love, so that you could release the pattern of attaching love to unhealthy behaviors that were completely unrelated to unconditional love. Perhaps your ex introduced you to AA or a spiritual center that propelled you into self-growth.

3. *Your ex reflected your childhood wounds, which enabled you to release them.* Maybe your ex-husband was inattentive just like your dad. Or your former boyfriend of seven years mirrored the abusive way your family treated you. Many of us have to re-experience those same traumas until we are able to say "enough" and move on from such patterns.
4. *He fathered your child.* I'm sure it's not the only reason, but sometimes I see couples getting together to create an amazing being. If you two were together for no other reason than to conceive a child who wouldn't otherwise exist, isn't that a miraculous reason to have been together?
5. *The torture of your bad relationship was bound to make your soulmate look extra good in your eyes.* People laugh when I say this in workshops, but I think it can be true. A big reason for you to have suffered through that really awful marriage may be so that when Ms. Right comes along, you will never take her for granted, and instead you will cherish your extraordinary match forever. In comparison to what you've been through before, you will always be grateful for what the two of you will share.

I don't mean to simplify. There are multiple reasons, some of which we will never know, to explain why we developed relationships with people who were not our soulmates. But even partially understanding why a particular relationship happened can aid us in letting it go. The thought that we get to go further on our journey, to more love than we've known before, also helps releasing come more easily.

It can delay opening up to your soulmate. No matter how badly you wanted a successful relationship with a past love, it will never happen with the wrong person. It will only work out with your soulmate. If you assume you're *not* holding on to someone, keep reading anyway. This information could be helpful to a friend, or perhaps by the end of the chapter, you may realize that you have a hidden attachment of which you are unaware.

Fewer than 10 percent of the participants in my *Releasing a Person* workshop later discover that the released person is truly their soulmate. Even if that person is their soulmate, the release exercise described later in this chapter may be the very piece of work that allows their soulmate to finally commit. You can't go wrong with release. Letting go is a very important process to master. As our lives continually evolve, we release the old to make space for the new.

The most obvious case of an attachment is a person who is still reeling from a breakup or divorce. I don't believe in real heartbreak—just a heart that is grieving and opening wider to love. However, if you were ever to characterize someone as brokenhearted, the following description would be it: the person mopes around, either trying to get away from their ex or taking steps to bump into them. He may call his ex's relatives to check up on the former flame, arrange to be where the ex will be, or avoid mutual friends. All of this behavior is done with the other person in mind, which means this person is still attached.

ATTACHMENT: FRIEND OR FOE?

Why do we grow to be so attached to another person? It is a tendency to emotionally glom on to someone, even before it's appropriate in dating. Psychologists have studied this phenomenon and discovered that attachment is necessary. Babies who are not allowed to attach to a parental figure will die. Bonding is essential to their well-being. A 1989 study concluded that the most important task of infancy is to develop a secure attachment with primary caregivers.[3] Adults, too, need attachments. Attachment keeps marriages together and from a spiritual perspective provides us with as close a glimpse of Oneness, the experience of the Divine, as we may ever feel. We are close to a love in more ways than to any other—physically, spiritually, emotionally, intellectually, and even on a soul level. I believe that this serves us. Attachment allows us to feel connected and to ensure that we have time to grow with someone we are involved with now, even if the person is not our soulmate. But when it's time to let go, we must release our former love so that we don't hang up our lives on something that is over. There is a time to say good-bye.

Saying good-bye is not easy, and some people would rather endure years of the torture that comes with hanging on than face the pain of a final release. The fact is that in our lifetime, we will have to say good-bye to every person we know, because we ultimately will leave this Earth one by one. Therefore, it behooves us all to improve our ability to release another person. The pain of letting go won't kill us, and it's better to get it over with and be ready for new love than to stick with old patterns or situations that aren't healthy for either person involved.

FIVE REASONS WHY LETTING GO IS THE SMART CHOICE

1. *Unrequited love is a frustrating waste of your time and energy.* You deserve more than someone who doesn't love you back wholeheartedly.
2. *Letting go has the opposite effect of what you might think.* Releasing a love is often the energy that pulls the person back to you, in what could be called a "rubber band effect" (though you need to think very carefully before getting back together.) What pushes people away is clinginess. (Please note that you don't want to make letting go a way of holding on, which can be a temptation. You need to let go, because it is the wise choice and creates a better energy in your life. Releasing is a great way to eradicate clinginess from your repertoire of acceptable behaviors or energies.)
3. *Letting go makes sure you are wide open to your soulmate.*

EMOTIONAL DAMAGE AND RELEASE

I find that the people who have the most difficult time releasing are those who are emotionally damaged. And there are very few of us who escaped childhood unscathed, thanks to a variety of societal beliefs at play when we were growing up. There seems to be a correlation between how damaged you are and how hard it is to let go. For example, a woman I worked with whose parent committed suicide when she was five years old was unable to release anyone

Holding on to a relationship that has run its course can distract you, delaying the advent of love into your life.

4. *Release is your first step into the life that's waiting for you.* While it may seem like an ending, letting go frees up a great deal of your energy, energy that was previously spent trying to hold on to someone who is not your soulmate. All of this unleashed energy will propel you into your next steps, which no doubt hold great promise for your future. Instead of being the *end* of something, you will one day look back and realize that the day you released your former love was the day you began your journey to *true* love.
5. *Release brings magic into your life.* It is a principle embraced by spiritual circles, twelve-step programs, and self-help groups alike. Letting go takes an act of faith, and you are rewarded for it in many ways.

she ever dated. She would avoid entire neighborhoods in her city where old flames lived. The few people you may know who are good at letting go are either the rare ones who grew up emotionally intact or those who have healed themselves through self-growth. We all can heal completely from past wounds.

If you are one of those people for whom letting go is excruciating, you need to do some emotional healing in addition to releasing.

FIVE STEPS TO EMOTIONAL HEALING

1. *Let the pain come up, and instead of fighting it, embrace it.* It won't kill you, so go ahead and feel your despair fully. Take some quiet time to explore your pain—even invite the pain in, so that you can explore it and heal it. You can do this daily as long as necessary. If you have a hard time bringing up the pain on command, try to make time for it as it arises. Cry as much as you can, as this is an important part of the release.
2. *Learn to disassociate from your pain.* Remove yourself from becoming your pain. Noticing when you get into a negative spiral of pain will help to dissolve it. Shining the light of your awareness into what you are feeling automatically removes you from it. How can you do this? When the pain arises, take a moment to notice it, and ask yourself what exactly you are feeling. By becoming aware of the pain, it can no longer take you over, and you get some distance from it. In situations when you can't afford to let your pain take you over, or when you just want to enjoy yourself and put the pain aside for a while, this technique of bringing attentiveness into the pain allows you to get beyond it and be present for what is needed in the moment. Practice this technique every time the pain appears.
3. *Practice not taking anything personally.* Train yourself to quit feeling pain when someone is unkind, rude, or dishonoring. Tell yourself, "He is showing himself to me, and saying nothing about *me* whatsoever. This has nothing to do with me." This will guard you against reinjury or reactivation of an old wound.
4. *When something begins to trigger your pain, try to identify exactly what you fear.* Instead of remaining in the fear,

explore how you would react if you replaced the fear with faith. If you knew everything would be okay, that you were Divinely supported, how would you react differently? Practice reacting in faith instead of fear and see how much easier life gets. A way to do so is to ask yourself, "What is it that I'm fearing right now?" Once you pinpoint the source of the pain, which is related to how you're interpreting the incident that triggered it, soothe yourself by telling yourself, "I'm okay, and since most of my fears are never realized, I'm not wasting another moment worrying about this." Then visualize the outcome that you *want* to have happen in the situation instead.

5. *Protect yourself by no longer allowing abuse or disrespect in your life*. Establish a zero tolerance policy for such negative behavior. For some, this may be quite a journey. Begin by becoming more aware of how you may allow anyone to treat you unkindly. Then be brave enough to draw boundaries against such treatment. A step as simple as saying "Please don't talk to me in that way" is tremendous progress. The goal here is to no longer injure your emotional being, thereby enlarging the pain you have been hanging on to. If the boundaries you put in place to guard against abuse or disrespect are disregarded, you need to become willing to enforce them either legally or by gaining distance from the abuser. This will take time if you've had a habit of allowing others to mistreat you, but keep working at it. The bottom line is that strictly enforcing your boundaries against bad treatment is something you have to do sooner or later, so be willing to tackle this issue now before any more of your life passes you by.

As you do this important work of releasing, and also healing the part of you that tends to hang on, you will see progress being made. For some, it happens very quickly, while for others, it is more of a process. Every time you make headway, make sure to congratulate yourself. Some people never learn to let go, and the fact that you are willing to tackle this big issue is a wonderful sign of your growth. It will serve you in many ways.

As I work with people in this area of heart decluttering, the two questions I hear most often are: (1) How do I know when I'm really over someone? and (2) How do I detach? The answers to these queries are critical to successfully completing this Magnetization Step.

HOW DO I KNOW WHEN I'M OVER HIM?

I have a litmus test in answer to this question: *when you can see your ex on a date with a new love or even kissing and you truly don't care, you're detached.* People groan when I say this, and I ask them a question: "How many of you have been in love before and gotten over it?" Most people raise their hands. Then, I ask: "So would it bother you to see that person kissing someone else?" They inevitably answer no. I point out that if you have ever gotten over anyone, you can get over *this* love, no matter how great you think the relationship was. This brings us to the question of the VofA (the "voice of attachment"), as I call it.

The Voice of Attachment (VofA)

- Attachment has its own voice that will tell you lies, but it makes them seem true.

- Attachment is like an addiction, and its voice is powerful while you are in its grip.
- Attachment will send you all kinds of messages. The most common one is: "This was the love of your life, the best love you've ever had. You will never have a love like this one again. This is your soulmate, and you have to make it work or love will pass you by for good."

Reality check: everyone in love always thinks that last thought. Everyone. Think back again to the past love that you got over. More than likely, you'll remember that you had this very thought about him before you detached. You thought that he was *it* for you. He was the love of your life, and you would never have another love like him. When you let go, these overdramatic thoughts do go away. And what I know above all else is that you do have more love in your future, better love, because the next time it will last. With your One, you won't have to let go, because it won't end.

Be very suspicious of any voice that makes it sound like you will die without this person or be condemned to a life of misery. The Voice of Attachment is needlessly dramatic and will set you back as you try to release past loves, so don't buy into it. Know it will fade as you successfully release. Whatever you do, don't make decisions based on the VofA. Ignore it, and make a decision only when you're in a centered, nondesperate state of mind. The VofA can get you all worked up, desperate. It is not good for you.

VofA Is Sneaky

The Voice of Attachment can be sneaky, working in strange ways, so beware. One common phenomenon is what I call the Stuff Syndrome. This is when you let any stuff, or possessions, you've left at each other's places get in the way of letting go. It is amazing how overly important these things become. And if it's not material things, then it's unfinished business like getting him to complete your Web site or giving him the name of your doctor that he's been asking for. I have seen people make up excuse after excuse to keep getting in touch with their previous partners, and at the time the reasons seem quite legitimate. But this is simply another way of holding on, propelled by the VofA. And embarrassingly, your ex knows what you're doing—he can see right through the excuses. The best course of action is to *not* feed the attachment, of course. How? Set aside his belongings in a box, and deliver them much later, when your attachment is gone. Better yet, have a friend drop them off (and don't quiz the friend when you see her later about if he asked about you and what he looked like). Find other ways of accomplishing your tasks that do not involve him. Don't fall into the Stuff Syndrome—it will only prolong your pain.

The Myth of Friendship

The VofA will also tell you that the two of you can be friends, even though it didn't work out. Right after the breakup of a relationship, there is no such thing as friendship, unless you are one of the evolved few. The VofA will insist that you two can be friends while secretly fanning the flames of hope that this will lead to reconciliation. You may even lower yourself to a "friends with benefits" situation (physical involvement while you're supposedly just being friends), which will only prolong your pain, adding insult to injury. Your best bet for losing the attachment is to gain as much distance as you can get, assiduously avoiding anything that will give you any hope about the relationship. Later on you can have a friendship, but not until your attachment is completely gone.

How do you know when the VofA is gone? The most common symptom is pondering your former love and asking yourself, "What was I *thinking*?" Then you know the grip of attachment is gone, and you're seeing clearly.

♥ MAGNETIZATION STEP 5 ♥
RELEASE IN THREE STAGES

To clear your energy for your soulmate, go through these three stages of releasing any former loves to whom you're still attached:

Stage One: Make up your mind that you're ready to release.
This is the most difficult step to take, because it is much easier to stay in denial that the relationship is not working out. You could go round and round with this decision for a few years, but I advise against it. While we all have our process, wasting years of your life because you refuse to let go makes no sense. You are putting your life on hold for someone with whom it will never work out.

It's true that you'll be in good company. I have seen hundreds of people who come to my *Releasing a Person* workshop once, only to appear again in the workshop a few years later to let go of the *exact same person*. They made the mistake of ignoring the initial release and giving the relationship another chance. In this work I've found that only a very small percentage of people who released are able to work it out with the person they let go of. A divorce lawyer told me a similar statistic. Approximately 10 percent of his clients end up reconciling with their partners. If you are tempted to conclude that you are one of these people, recognize again the Voice of Attachment trying to seduce you, and refuse to let it sway you.

I have noticed that release has been good even for those scant few who ultimately end up with their ex. The release experience is powerful enough to give your former partner room to see that she's the One. She literally feels you releasing her and responds. However, don't try to fake your release to win back a former love—faking it doesn't work. It doesn't have the same energy.

Hopefully I've persuaded you to take this all-important step and decide that, yes, it is high time to let go of your former love to free yourself for soulmate love. If you are ready and willing to move on, if you have really made up your mind to release, then write the following statement in your Soulmate Journal: "I now set the intention to release [your *ex's name*]." After you have written it down, stand up and say these words aloud with conviction.

Stage Two: Create a release ritual for yourself.

If you think of weddings, funerals, and even graduations, you realize how powerful rituals can be. It helps to invite a trusted friend or two over to witness this rite of passage for the relationship (or if you are doing the Ten-Week Soulmate Magnetization Program in appendix 1, you will do this with the group). It almost doesn't matter what you do in the ritual as long as you are saying good-bye. See the box titled "An Effective Release Ritual" for an example of a helpful process.

To get ready for the ritual, get a photo of your ex or the two of you together. Light a candle or two, and in your own way, say good-bye. Talk about the highs and lows of the relationship, tell him why you're angry, and ultimately say: "[*Your ex's name*], I release you"—and mean it. Let yourself cry if you need to afterward.

After you finish this ritual, record in your Soulmate Journal how you are feeling and why it was best to release, plus any revelations you had in the process of letting go.

Stage Three: Use tools to keep releasing as necessary.

For many people, the letting go ritual described in Stage Two is enough. They feel complete with their previous relationship and never look back. For others, the release proves to be more of a process. You may feel initially free of your ex and excited to move on, only to find yourself slipping back into thinking of him. If you're sliding into the old attachment, your release will take a bit longer and be more of a gradual letting go. For you, there are three powerful tools that will aid you in continuing to release.

AN EFFECTIVE RELEASE RITUAL

This outline of a ritual can be adjusted to your own spiritual beliefs or situation. Use it as a guide, but feel free to tailor it. For example, you can hold a cross in your hand if you're Christian, or incorporate another tradition like Judaism or Buddhism practice into it. The listener is taken through a similar process in my *Releasing a Person* CD.

- *Pull out the photo of your ex and sit with it in front of the lighted candle.*
- *While looking at the photo, connect with your ex on a soul (not a personality) level.* What does this mean? Put aside any hatred, any grief feelings on your part, and overlook anything about him that is difficult for you, and find the pure connection of love that is underneath. Say "hello."
- *Allow yourself to remember your time together.* First think of the good times, such as your first meeting, your first kiss, the first time you were physically intimate, the process of falling in love, and all that you have shared.
- *Now think of the bad times when it hurt, when you realized it was falling apart, when you felt alone.*
- *Let yourself become conscious of the reality of the relationship, what was true about it.* Beyond your hopes and dreams, beyond the fantasy, what was your relationship, and what was it not? For example, one man felt that his ex-girlfriend was his true love, despite the fact that she repeatedly told him she wasn't in love with him. His realization during this step was that she never really loved him (something he was in denial about), and that she wasn't his One after all. Ask yourself what the gifts of this relationship were.

- *Now take a moment to forgive him, even if it's difficult.* Remember that he was doing the best he could and that you were not a victim, as you chose to stay longer than you should have. Know that harboring resentment and anger only hurts you, so be willing to forgive, even if it's difficult.
- *Forgive yourself for anything you blame yourself for in the relationship.* You, too, were doing the best you could, and you are only human.
- *Vow to take away any lessons you received, and to not repeat any mistakes you made here.*
- *It is now almost time to say good-bye.* Before you do, take a moment to silently say any last words you have to say to your ex.
- *Once you've finished saying your piece, allow a moment of inner listening to see if there are any last words that your ex would like to say to you.* You very well may hear something, since you two are still connected on a soul level.
- *Now, with one last energetic hug, release this person on several different planes of being (physical, emotional, mental, spiritual).* Imagine cutting any ties between the two of you so that you can be free. Feel the connection leaving you. If any tears come up, let them flow. Embrace whatever feelings are aroused in you. And if you feel empty, that's good. The emptiness means you have released your former love and now have a sacred space within you, a vacuum that you want to protect and preserve for your soulmate.

Three Tools for Continued Release

1. *Let go moment-by-moment, day-by-day.* You may think of him a thousand times a day or more when you first break up. Every single time you catch yourself thinking of him, do a quick release. Say aloud (or silently if you're in public): "[*Your ex's name*], I release you to your highest good." Take a moment to feel the release. Understand that being willing to release is a magical energy. Every time you have the courage to let go, something good will happen to support you. I've seen the magic of this, and it's amazing. No matter how many times a day you have to do it, keep letting go each time you feel the attachment rearing its head.
2. *After you release, turn your focus back to the vision you have for your own life.* Perhaps the reason this works so well is that we seek in another what we fear we lack in ourselves. Therefore, rather than looking outside yourself for something, turn your thoughts to yourself to reduce your attachment feelings. As you take your attention off of your ex and begin looking forward by contemplating your own life and what you want in it, the pain tends to go away. Spend some time pondering this thought: "If I could have anything I wanted, if my life could look just the way I want it, what would it be like?" Include in the vision for your life not only your soulmate, but even career plans, life purpose, where you live, and how you live. Don't limit yourself. Think big.
3. *Deal with your "pain body"* appropriately. Eckhardt Tolle's breakthrough best seller, *The Power of Now,* devotes a whole chapter to the "pain body." The pain body, as Tolle

describes it, is the accumulation of all the pain and hurts you've had in your life and never dealt with. It will be activated at the time of a breakup. Because of this, you can tend to be a drama queen, crying all over your friends and family until they're at wit's end. While it is necessary to deal with your pain (because ignoring it, anesthetizing it, or suppressing it doesn't work), you should do so appropriately for your own sake as well as that of others. This means allowing yourself time to cry and grieve each day while being able to function as needed the rest of the time. I've found that the shower is a wonderful place to cry, because it's private. You have time to think about your grief, and the water is already flowing. You can also set aside a time to lock yourself away for a good daily cry. This is important to honor your grieving process.

Even though it may feel that way, our lives don't end just because we've had a horrible breakup. Therefore, we must find a way to continue functioning. Most of us have work or kids to deal with and don't have the option of checking out of life for a while. Confronting and dealing with your pain body, rather than ignoring it, will help you release more quickly. It will also begin the healing of the cumulative pain body, the pain you've carried around long before this present breakup. As you continue this work, you can dissolve the pain body entirely and it will no longer hinder you in your life.

Use these three tools daily as long as necessary. You may not need them for long or at all, but if you do, you'll notice a gradual lessening of the attachment until one day you're completely over it and happily engaged in your life without pain.

SPECIAL CIRCUMSTANCES: I HAVE TO SEE HER REGULARLY

Some people don't have the luxury of distance after a breakup or divorce. Physical and emotional distance and space from your ex is a great way to let go more quickly. However, if the two of you have children together, work together, or have other reason to see each regularly, space is not an option. What can you do?

First, I feel that people who are given a circumstance like this must be up to the task or it wouldn't fall on them. They must release at deeper levels. Realize that *you are more than this situation* and that the Universe will help you handle it.

Second, minimize contact that doesn't have to do with the issues at hand (children, work). It would be easy to let your Voice of Attachment go wild, but this won't help anything. Keep your interactions with your ex to practical matters. Let the rest go.

Ways to avoid seeing your ex more often than necessary include:

- Arranging to pick up the children at school rather than having to see each other in the process.
- Communicating through a third party when possible: a mediator, your assistant, a colleague, a lawyer, a mutual friend (try the others first, because this is a difficult position to put a friend in).
- When you do see each other, keeping it strictly busi-

ness. Don't drag out old grievances, break down, or get personal.

Even when your ex is in your life on a daily basis, it is possible to stay detached. Use the tools given early in this chapter for continued release as much as you need to.

DEALING WITH ANGER OVER AN EX

I asked you to forgive in the earlier release ritual, and there was a good reason. A subset of breakups involves the angry feelings (actually covering up hurt) that can result and the need for forgiveness. Some of us are extraordinarily good at hanging on to the injustice of it all. We can even revel in playing the victim. This serves no one, least of all you. It's certainly bad for your love life. Think of the stereotypical date where one person spends the whole time complaining about his ex. You don't want to be this person. More good reasons to resolve your anger and forgive are:

- There's probably plenty of blame to go around. Even if you were a victim, you're probably responsible for staying even after you got the first warning signs that this person was hurtful to you. This is not to blame you as the victim, particularly if the relationship was deeply abusive, it is just to point out that you had a part in drawing out the situation by not leaving at the first sign of trouble.
- Your ex was doing the best that he could. If he could have been more charitable, more fair, or more

honest, he would have. No doubt he will suffer for this behavior repeatedly until he reaches the point where he can heal his own wounds. You may not even be aware of the experiences he has gone through that caused him to behave as he did. Again, if you were in an abusive relationship, this is not to excuse the perpetrator. But understanding that the other person has pain will make it easier for you to forgive and get on with your life.

- If you can't forgive in order to be charitable to him, do it for yourself. Your former love is not affected by your anger as much as you are. To carry around bitterness means you're missing out on the joy and fun you could be experiencing. You're putting your life on hold for a grudge.
- If you're angry at yourself, get over it. To aid in forgiving yourself, understand that you did the best you could. While you can apologize if necessary, your guilt will serve no one. I believe that at a deep level there are no mistakes. You can't destroy a relationship with the right person. Accept that it wasn't meant to be, and quit beating yourself up over it, as doing so serves no purpose. While forgiving yourself may not be easy, catch yourself every time you begin to berate yourself, and say silently to yourself: "I was doing the best I could. I'm not a bad person, and I forgive myself." You may even need to sit down with your Soulmate Journal and list the reasons that you were doing the best you could, but keep working at releasing any self-anger until it is completely gone.

- Give up the notions of rejection and of being dumped. Both are false. Love is simply not regulated by logic and never will be. You can't blame someone for no longer being in love with you, nor should you waste time throwing stones because he left you to be with someone else. There is no reason in love. Keep telling yourself that until you can put aside a tendency to be bitter. One day, not too far away, the lack of logic in love will work in your favor, as we will discuss further in chapter 8 on dating.

There are certain therapies that have proven useful in dealing with anger and being able to forgive. I highly recommend the book *The Dance of Anger*, by Harriet Lerner, and also *Forgiveness Is a Choice*, by Robert D. Enright. You may also need to find a counselor who specializes in Gestalt therapy or anger management, or you can join an anger management group. Holding on to anger is a serious issue, and you have too much joy and love waiting for you to stay mad. If anger was your model growing up, it is an emotional pattern that is deeply ingrained, and you may very well need some help to give up this pattern. Often, this simple process for forgiveness is sufficient:

- Write down all of your grievances.
- Hit a pillow a few times while voicing the hurt.
- Write and verbalize why you forgive your ex.

When you show willingness to forgive, even when it's difficult, you introduce grace into the situation, and it frees you from bad feelings. Practice forgiveness every day so that it becomes second nature. This can be difficult for you if you've never practiced it before. Like many of us, you may have to train yourself to forgive, but the rewards are many.

MORE SUBTLE ATTACHMENTS AND KEEPING YOUR LOVE CUP EMPTY

You may have read this chapter and concluded, "I'm in good shape—I have no unhealthy attachments, so this is not me." But please realize there are more subtle levels of attachment. You may be hanging on to someone without knowing it. When you are single, your "love cup" can be pretty empty. You miss the emotional and physical closeness of being in a relationship, and this creates a void. And there is a tendency to want to fill this emptiness with something—what I refer to as filling your "love cup." The most common cup filler is a past love. You may find yourself daydreaming about your first love, wondering what it would be like if you two had married. Or you may compare every new date with a former love. This is not the agonized attachment of a new breakup, but it is still attachment, nonetheless. It is much easier to imagine a past love, someone known, than to anticipate something that's not yet on the horizon, your soulmate.

It bears repeating: *Don't try to fill up your love cup with a past love.* The best plan is to guard your love cup's emptiness at all costs. You want to save the space in your heart for your One. Some people are not very comfortable with an empty love cup. It can feel lonely or even bereaved, especially if you're emotionally wounded. But I want you to label your empty love cup "good." It is a treasure to be guarded and not filled up with anything but your true love. While you do need to keep your heart open, avoid any desperate acts prompted by the emptiness of the space in your heart that you are saving for your love. There is a difference between casually falling back into intimacy with someone you know isn't right and opening to love from a centered, content energy.

To keep the sacredness of your empty love cup safe for your One, you must empty it of anyone you've been putting in there, even without knowing it. At some of my workshops I lead a guided meditation in which participants must imagine their soulmates. It's amazing how many people put a face on their soulmate, and it's always the face of a past love. Until that moment they weren't aware that they were hanging on to their ex, but as a result of the meditation exercise they realize they're still attached to that person. Examine your heart, and if you find that you're still attached to anyone from your past (and know this is a very human tendency), release her in the way I've explored in this chapter.

THE REBOUND REFLEX

Emily, a former client, wrote me:

> *Always listen to your inner voice. I didn't and I paid the price. I had gone through a pretty rough breakup (even when you know it's over, it's still difficult). Anyway, I convinced myself to just go in the complete opposite direction. I met someone and could not have been less attracted to him. He is a good person, don't get me wrong, but not my soulmate. I ignored my inner voice and married him anyway. We are now divorced.*

EXERCISE:

DO YOU HAVE SUBCONSCIOUS ATTACHMENTS?

Are you attached to someone without knowing it? If you answer yes to any of these questions, you need to do some releasing.

1. Do you cringe when you hear news of your ex with a new love?
2. Do you either completely avoid his neighborhood or often drive by his house?
3. Do you hang on to words of hope your mutual friend said about your ex's new romance, such as, "It's a rebound relationship. It won't last"?
4. When she is at a party, do you have heightened awareness about where she is during most of the event?
5. Do you compare new people you are dating to your old flame, wondering if anyone will ever measure up?
6. If anyone asks you about your love history, do you dwell on this relationship, telling way more of the story than is needed?
7. Are you still upset with your ex? Do you relish hearing bad things about him or harbor resentments against him?

It is a natural inclination to have a rebound relationship. Emily made the mistake of marrying hers. Because there are no rules in love, sometimes the person you become involved with in a rebound relationship turns out to be the One. But far too often such relationships are entered into simply for comfort. Another name used for a rebound relationship in psychological circles is *transition relationship*. Clearly this phenomenon is common enough that it has more than one name.

A rebound relationship can be a gift, one that nurtures you through a difficult time, but you need to be careful. You run the risk of hurting the other person, which is unkind at best. Honesty is the proper policy, so that he can decide for himself whether he can deal with the situation at hand. You're also in danger of filling your love cup with the wrong person, for the wrong reasons. Only rarely does a transition person turn out to be your One. Being aware and following your intuition, which Emily didn't do, are necessary to navigate your way through a rebound relationship.

My test for measuring the rightness of a rebound relationship is asking yourself this question: "As I get better, back on my feet, do I feel like I still want this person, or am I just hanging on to him for a sense of comfort? Is this a feeling of romantic love that I have, or is it more of an emotional neediness that he is filling?"

CRAZY LOVE

The phenomenon of "crazy love," an unbalanced and dramatic attachment, is one I mentioned earlier, in chapter 1. What does being in this kind of relationship reveal about you? Perhaps nothing more than that you got highly involved with the *wrong* person, someone who can't make you happy and pushes every button you have. However, if you've had a checkered past full of unbalanced relationships, you have some serious inner work to do. You may be addicted to drama, which prohibits you from being in a real, deep relationship. You may allow yourself to get bored easily with a stable, nondramatic person. If this is the case, you need to start seeing love relationships differently. This section will help you to choose a new way of being.

How do you change your tendency toward crazy love? First, recognize the "exciting" partners who you are drawn to as being unstable, bad relationship material, crazy-making, and unattractive to someone who wants her soulmate. Next, force yourself to date a new type of person. Your dates should still be attractive to you, but look for stable, nondramatic sorts.

Violet had a pattern of dating addictive types, from alcoholics to smokers, even to cocaine addicts. She found them exciting and didn't realize until after she'd become emotionally involved that they were addictive. Finally, with Adam, she had had enough. Yes, he was sexy, charming, in a rock band. But he used cocaine and other substances regularly. Violet delivered an ultimatum to him: "Go on another binge, and I'm out of here." She meant it. Sure enough, a few months later Adam was up all night, bouncing off the walls, a guaranteed sign of coke use. Violet immediately broke up with him. It pained her to do it, but she had vowed to find a healthier way.

As she grieved the loss of Adam, Violet examined why she

needed this sort of relationship. In therapy she realized that her dad had been an alcoholic and that she had somehow plugged an addictive personality into her definition of what was lovable. She worked hard to reframe what love meant to her, replacing her old idea of being a loving enabler with a picture of a healthy, equal relationship. The therapy process was not easy for her. It brought up much grief about the painful childhood she had endured and the reality of how little she had accepted for herself as an adult.

Violet had a tough time getting over Adam but kept turning down dates with anyone who was similar to him, until Chris came into her life. Handsome and interesting, he was also stable and low-key compared to anyone she had ever dated. It took awhile to get used to the lack of drama, but the longer Violet dated Chris, the harder she fell. They are married today and have the life that Violet had always wanted, one that is rich, deep, and endlessly loving.

Crazy love is draining and demands your focus, to the detriment of other areas of your life. Your friends are probably sick of hearing it. One incident that finally made me break up with a crazy love partner was when a friend said to me, "I'm really tired of hearing about it. He puts you through the wringer, and it's painful to hear. Why do you stay?" Once you give up the crazy love, you will have more emotional resources to balance your life. Further, in a non-crazy love relationship, you will go deeper with your partner, having a richer, more romantic relationship than you could with all of the drama. It is very rare that a crazy love is a soulmate connection (though it may feel that way—the excitement can be alluring). If you two are able to put the drama aside and do the self-growth work necessary to get through your problems and find stability, you may be soulmates. (See chapter 10 for particular suggestions on how to grow beyond the drama of crazy love.) But if this fails, or if your partner is not willing to meet you halfway in dealing with his issues, he probably is not your soulmate, and you need to put this relationship behind you.

BEING IN THE MOMENT

There is such a thing as love in the moment. The slightest interaction with another person can be sacred. Some of your dalliances along the way to your soulmate can be short but can still feed your soul. Some affairs of the heart are meant only for a moment in your life, and it's good to understand this. If it's not working out right now with the person you are attached to, you must release him or her to free yourself for what *is* right for you now. If you are willing to listen, you can ask your intuition and know exactly when it's over and time to release.

What does this mean, practically speaking? It means you don't need to try to make a fling or even a one-night stand into something more. Since we humans have such a tendency to get attached, it's possible that you may erroneously latch on to someone with whom you were meant to share only a lovely moment or two. If this is the case, the moment you realize it's not working out, do the release work outlined earlier in this chapter, and be willing to accept this short relationship for the quick love that it was.

RELEASING AFTER A DEATH

One compelling reason to let go is that we must ultimately say good-bye to every person we love on this Earth. I've mentioned it before, but it bears repeating. It behooves us to become competent at letting go, because our lives are a series of releasing people. For this reason, I find letting go to be one of the most useful tools we can ever learn. The constant good-byes are also a good motive to live fully, loving with your whole heart, because only such a full life can defray the pain of losing loved ones as they leave our life.

When someone dies, even someone you consider to be your soulmate, you must let go. Why? Because you're still here, and he's not. He has gone on to whatever is next for him, and you must do the same, here on Earth. This is difficult to do, but to live the rest of your days as a tragic figure of loss turns you into a victim and does not honor the life you still have to live. Even if you've been with a spouse for many years, you must learn what your life is to be now. The people I've seen who have the hardest time letting go are the extremely young and those who were married for decades. Why? Because to some extent, they may have made their love partner the source of all their happiness. They haven't learned that there is always more love, and that losing this one person isn't the end of love for them. The truth is that there is always more love and that releasing even the most amazing love is not the end of love for you. You have more love to experience for as long as you live.

A FINAL, IMPORTANT QUESTION ABOUT RELEASING

Q: So how released from past loves do I have to be to allow my soulmate into my life?

A: Ideally, you should be completely released from your past relationships. However, I have seen people with just a corner of an opening in their hearts, and this is enough room for their soulmate to enter. It is even possible that your soulmate will help you to do the last bit of releasing needed.

Whatever the case may be, you can't go wrong with releasing. Practice it and become proficient at it. You can use it as a dating tool when a relationship isn't working out, and this skill will serve you for the rest of your life. Best of all, the act of releasing unleashes a quality of magic in your life that is tangible. It is an act of surrender, and you are rewarded for it every time.

I affirm that you are now free and clear, wide open for love. You are well able to continue releasing past loves as needed, and you see the clear support of the Universe as you walk forward. Your emotional healing to wholeness is well under way.

6

A Delicate Time

The Sixth Magnet: Create a Haven for Your Heart

As you open up to this new paradigm of love and soulmates, you are in a delicate state. Being single is to be inherently vulnerable, and as you read this book you are undergoing changes, some of which you may be unaware. A subtle process is taking place within you. This transformation makes you more emotionally fragile than usual. Why? When we learn something new, there is a period of time between *realization,* when you have an a-ha moment as you grasp a new view or concept, and *embodiment,* the time when you accept the new viewpoint, have no doubt about its truth, and have adjusted your life and world to accommodate the view.

As you realize that your idea of dating and what you could hope for in love have been limited and start believing you really do have a soulmate, you are in a vulnerable state. Any naysayer can quash your hope. One bad date can shoot you into despair. Eventually there comes a time when you are strong in your belief in love. This is easier when you are in your love's arms, but many people I work with come to be sure they have a soulmate before their One actually appears. This certainty saves them from going through dating and singles hell.

Until you have developed a rock-solid belief in soulmates and love, understand that you need to protect yourself. During this critical period of inner growth, it's easy to get knocked down by the first strong wind of negativity. You need to guard against anyone raining on your parade. It's also a good idea to develop effective ways to strengthen yourself when you're having a difficult time. Below are some methods to both shelter and fortify yourself.

♥ MAGNETIZATION STEP 6 ♥
LEARN TO PROTECT AND STRENGTHEN YOURSELF

There are many steps you can take to protect and strengthen yourself as you open your heart to love. Read through the following two lists, "Ways to Shelter Yourself" and "Ways to Stay Strong," and decide which suggestions are most needed in your life. In your Soulmate Journal, list the steps you will take to protect and strengthen yourself.

Ways to Shelter Yourself

- Dismiss the naysayers. Distance yourself from friends and family who play into your worst fears about love and feed into your insecurities. The grandpa who says, "You're not getting any younger, better catch a husband while you can," needs to be avoided.
- *Train people what* not *to say to you.* If you can't or don't want to distance yourself from someone who is important to you, there's another option. You can ask friends and family not to mention certain aspects of your life that stir your vulnerabilities. This may sound difficult, but the other option is to cut them out of your life for now, while you're vulnerable, or limit contact with them. Examples:

Mom: Honey, you're not even dating. How will you ever find the right person?
You: Mom, it's really hard on me when you judge my love life. If you can't say anything positive, let's just not discuss it, okay? We have lots of other things to talk about.

Friend: God, another date that crashed and burned. How long before you just give up on love entirely?
You: Do you realize how negative that sounds? I really need you to be supportive of me. Saying something like "You're one date closer to Mr. Right" would be more helpful. Please help me to stay positive, okay?

Ex-boyfriend: That dude was a loser. Have you gotten that desperate?
You: Do you realize how hurtful that is? I would appreciate your not making any more negative comments and being nice instead.

- *Limit what you read and watch on television.* I have a single client who goes into deep depression every time there is a news story highlighting how pitiful singles are in one way or another. Myths that the media perpetuate include how difficult it is to be single, how few good men are left, and the insurmountable odds of meeting someone. Get in touch with yourself to know what hits your nerve of insecurity, and avoid exposure to these reports.
- *Avoid places that weaken you—limit your risk taking.* Unfortunately, some singles events have an air of desperation. This will set you back, and it's doubtful you'll meet anyone surrounded with that cloud. Psychology writer David Weiner points out that our brains have a primitive social dominance system that wants us to "play it safe."[4] While the ultimate goal is to learn to take bigger risks and expand the parameters in which you feel safe, it's okay to limit yourself to situations where you feel comfortable as you work on your self-esteem. Until then, don't feel a need to push yourself. It's fine to limit the social risks you take until you feel stronger.

Ways to Stay Strong

Beyond simply sheltering yourself, you can also shore yourself up, keeping your energy high and your thoughts positive. Here are some devices for keeping yourself in a good place:

- *Look for great love stories to give you hope.* Ask long-married couples how they met. Sniff out against-all-odds tales of people getting together despite distance, age, or appearance.
- *Journal during difficult moments.* Journaling has been quite beneficial to people who are in periods of heightened growth as they open to love. Writing down your thoughts and experiences can help you come to terms with them. It is a therapeutic method often suggested by mental health professionals. I teach the following system for dealing with difficult moments:
    - Write down everything you are feeling at the moment, even if it's ugly or profane. Spare no words.
    - Once you have it all down, you should feel a release.
    - Go back and look over what you're written to reframe it.
    - Realize that what you wrote was your view of the moment, but not a reality.
    - Take each negative thought and write down a positive truth from it, one that is the opposite of it.

Example: You write: "I am always going to be single. Rejection follows me everywhere I go." Your affirmation would be: "My singles days are coming to an end. There is no rejection. God is just closing the doors that are not my path, because up ahead there is a wide-open door to the most amazing love I could ever imagine."

It doesn't work to ignore your difficult feelings, but once you give them some room to express, you can remind yourself of what is true.

> *Stay centered by meditating, praying, reading inspiring literature, or doing yoga.*

AN AFFIRMATIVE PRAYER FOR YOUR LOVE LIFE

I am a big believer in prayer, and during times of stress I'm so glad that I use it routinely as a tool. I feel that affirmative prayer (praying as though you believe something has already been given to you) is more powerful than any other. Here is a prayer you can say whenever your doubts about love surface.

God, thank you for my soulmate, whom I affirm is coming to me even now. I bless him wherever he is and trust that we are brought together in the perfect time. As I say this prayer, he feels it and is also uplifted. I release any doubt in my heart or mind that I get love, for love is my divine inheritance. I have faith in You and in love. Thy will be done. I give thanks for this precious gift. Amen

- *Draw closer to those friends and family members who support you as you open up to your love.* If they make you feel good and don't tear you down, turn to them.
- *Be romantic in your everyday life.* Light candles of hope to remind you of your love, buy sexy lingerie to feel romance-ready.
- *Practice flirting with whoever's around to keep yourself feeling attractive, the juices flowing.*
- *Remember all the odd ways you met someone in the past.*
- *Remind yourself of how you are attractive and desirable and how anyone would be lucky to have you.*
- *Get in the practice of connecting with your love on inner levels, even before you have met, by thinking of him and sending him love.*

After you have listed in your Soulmate Journal which of the above steps you want to take to protect and strengthen yourself, do three of them right away. In the coming days, refer back to your journal often to remind yourself of the haven you are building in your life for your heart. During particularly difficult moments, go back to this list and find an activity that will help you.

IT'S TIME TO RECEIVE

I find that many people who are still learning to shelter themselves properly during vulnerable times are lousy at receiving. They're good at giving to others but fall short in being able to accept help and support. If this sounds like you, part of protecting yourself is to gravitate toward those friends and family members who give to you and then *let them love you*. For some, this can be difficult. If you've been challenged at accepting help, support, and gifts from others, you are out of whack. We must all have balance in our lives, and the healthiest people and relationships are those that involve an equal measure of giving and receiving.

If you tend to attract friends who are *takers*, who expect you to give to them or make your relationship all about them, now is a good time to distance yourself from those people. Here are some signs that a relationship is not good for you:

- You feel exhausted after you see your friend. Some people can suck all of the life out of you, or even out of the room.
- You often find yourself agitated when dealing with the person.
- It feels as though you give and this person takes, a one-way street.

If this is what the relationship looks like, it is not an equal friendship and is especially not good for you at this stage in your life. It is a bit of a "using" situation. There are two courses of action necessary to free up your life from this energy drain:

1. *Try to change the relationship.* Draw some boundaries about how much you can be there for your friend. And further, ask for your friend's support by determining

whether she is able to listen to you and offer emotional support for *your* problems. Ask for a favor and see how your friend or love responds. It is possible that you are so used to giving, you forget to even attempt to lean on others. Many people would love a chance to do something for you, and perhaps you just haven't given them the opportunity. If this strategy works, you can save the friendship and make it more balanced.

2. *If the first strategy fails and your friend is appalled at the thought of listening to you and supporting you, it's time to release her or at least distance yourself for now.* First, do an inner release by making a decision that this friendship is not serving you. Next, a direct "breakup" with a problematic friend can be good and healthy. If you have problems with being direct, it's probably better for you to deal with the problem head-on. Yes, this can be stressful, but it is good practice for you in drawing boundaries, something most people who avoid confrontation find difficult. However, if you don't feel strong enough to tackle such growth during this vulnerable time, simply make yourself unavailable, don't return phone calls, allow some distance to set in. You can gradually drift apart until you are completely free from this draining relationship.

To let yourself be run into the ground by unequal friendships shows a lack of self-esteem. It is critical that you take action to get yourself away from relationships that tear you down. Only you can make the decision to allow friendships that nurture you both.

HOLIDAY HELL

I remember from my single days how tough holidays could be, especially Valentine's Day, major family holidays like Christmas, and New Year's. These are times when emotional suffering can be intensified. Those who are single are reminded that they don't have romance and often feel left out. In my workshops, people often ask, "What can I do to get through Valentine's [or another holiday] easier?" Here are some suggestions for ensuring that holidays are not just bearable but even enjoyable as a solo activity:

1. If you are dreading Valentine's Day or another holiday, *find faith in your heart that you* will *get love and that love is on the way.* No matter how old, young, out of shape, or unattractive you think you are, there is someone for you. Your soulmate will not be able to see past you, and will think you are the most special person on Earth. Remember this, and affirm that your love is coming. Doing so will make the holiday much more bearable.
2. *Release your embarrassment about being single.* It is amazing how many people are vaguely ashamed to show up at my workshops. They're mortified to admit that they are unattached, as though it were a sin. This attitude is misguided. We all are single in our lives at some point, and this is an important stage, not to be missed. Everyone is single for at least a few Valentine's Days, and being without a love relationship shouldn't be cause for shame. If you find yourself single on any holiday, understand that that's okay. People are not judging you and probably aren't noticing who is single and who is not.

Most folks are too self-absorbed to focus on your single status, unless they are responding to your energy field that might as well be a sign on your back: "Ashamed of Being Solo." As you release your own judgments, you will find yourself free to enjoy your holidays.

3. *Remember that once you are with your One, it will heal every bad Valentine's Day you ever had.* You will be too busy being happy in the arms of your soulmate to even remember the difficult holidays. All sorts of things you had been missing, such as a romantic date, flowers, candy, gifts of jewelry, poems, and passionate love-making, will be made up for in the most delicious way.
4. To open yourself to love, even though your soulmate is not here yet, *go shopping for* or *make a card, a very romantic card* (we talked about this in the process of sending out your soul call, and a holiday is a great time to do it). Have fun completing this task and revel in the fact that one day very soon, you'll be able to give it to your true love. Once you have the card, put it in a special place. Save it until your love arrives, and give it to him at the right time.
5. On Valentine's Day and other holidays, *send love to the soulmate you haven't yet met,* a person who is living and breathing somewhere right now. Understand that this person doesn't have their One for this occasion either, but soon enough you will be together to celebrate this day.
6. *Plan* now for what you will do on the holiday. Don't be alone at home, where you can feel isolated. Make dinner plans with a good friend or a group of friends. Or do something loving for someone you know who is also alone.

MY FAVORITE NEW YEAR'S EVE

I have a group of friends who like to call ourself "The Gang." Several of us were going through a divorce at the same time and began hanging out to learn to cope with our newly single status. None of us had New Year's Eve dates, so we decided to have a slumber party at our friend Craig's large house. We played poker, pool, and Truth or Dare and relaxed in the hot tub. After ringing in the new year, we all changed into pajamas and found a bed to sleep in. The next morning, one of the guys made French toast and coffee, and we watched football and the Twilight Zone marathon all day while playing cards. It was my favorite New Year's Eve of all time, and I've had some good ones. To this day, The Gang and I are still good friends, and they are the ones who introduced me to my husband and soulmate, Jon. It has been a pleasure to watch each one of The Gang find love one by one.

7. *If you are going through heartbreak through the holidays, take especially good care of yourself.* Release your ex, and don't let your loneliness exacerbate the longing. Firmly remind yourself that the relationship ended for a reason, and daydream about the soulmate you will soon meet. This is healthier. Go back to chapter 5 and work on your tools for releasing as needed.
8. *Don't make a date with someone you're not into, just to*

have something to do. This will just make you feel worse. Better to be with the friends you know and enjoy.

TURN YOUR BACK ON NEGATIVITY

Negativity is quite commanding—and demanding. Its energy is attention-getting. You can be in a room full of happy, chattering people, and if a fight breaks out, the place will go silent, with all eyes riveted on the conflict. Learning how to avoid negativity is deep work. We are taught how to look for the hurt, the criticism, or the potential threat rather than focusing on the happiness and the kindness in everyday life. Being on guard for antagonism is a misguided attempt to protect ourselves. Remember: what you focus on becomes bigger. So the more you look for the hurt, the more you will find it.

The best way to avoid negativism is to pay it no attention. This can be difficult. But as you starve it from your attention, focusing instead on the positive, the support, the love in your life, your world experience will change. This is one of the keys to protecting yourself as you open to love. As you learn the power of staying positive, you evoke an amazing magnetism in your life that will bring not only love, but many other good things as well. It serves as its own protection.

Positive thinking can literally change your brain chemistry, your reality, according to David Weiner.[5] Weiner says that practices such as focusing on positive thoughts will change your brain structures, but repetition is vital to success. It takes perseverance to learn how to be positive in the face of great adversity, but the payoff is worth it. A study at the University of Wisconsin found that people who concentrated on positive thoughts were healthier and had more immunity to bacterial and viral illnesses.[6] In addition, studies show that optimists tend to live longer and experience less stress than pessimists or realists.[7] If there were ever a time to work on being more positive, this is it.

KATHRYN'S QUICK TIPS FOR ERADICATING NEGATIVITY

- When you find yourself focusing or even obsessing on something negative, interrupt your thoughts.
- In your Soulmate Journal, write down what happened, what you are feeling, and why you are feeling that way.
- Now turn it around. Remind yourself of the positive aspect of the situation or why it's not as big a deal as you're making it out to be (i.e,. Betty said something unkind. Remind yourself that what she said is just her opinion and tells you more about *her* thoughts than anything about you.) Find an optimistic outlook for this situation, and write it down in your journal. You are retraining your brain with a different way of dealing with negativity in this process.
- Once you've finished journaling, turn your thoughts away from the negativity and focus instead on something constructive. If the thoughts keep reappearing, allow yourself some more processing time (through journaling as described above), and then once again guide your thoughts elsewhere.

THE MYTH OF "DOOMED FOR ALL OF ETERNITY"

As humans, we have a tendency to "catastrophize" our misfortunes into a drama beyond what is warranted. This must be why I hear so often, "I'm sure that I'm doomed to walk the Earth single for the rest of my days." Please. Have you ever thought this or said it? Catastrophizing is a way to inflict abuse on ourselves, and it behooves you to learn to release this pattern of drama.

I have had people tell me they are the last one among their friends to get married, and they are sure this means they will never have love. The truth is that, unfortunately, almost half of their friends' marriages may be doomed to failure according to current divorce statistics. When you're in catastrophic thinking, you may behave in ways that are not in alignment with your path, putting yourself in that same situation where divorce is likely. A moment of drama, particularly a self-created one, is the worst time to make decisions. You may marry for the wrong reason or settle for dating someone who does not excite you.

The truth beyond this doom-and-gloom thinking is this:

> This moment is just a snapshot of your life as it is today. It is not a life sentence for you. Times will get better. If you feel behind in your life, like most of your friends have married or hooked up and you are left behind, know that you will catch up and perhaps surpass them in terms of the quality of relationship you will have. Even in what may look like a dating desert, there is love for you out there beyond any momentary appearance.

Rather than beat yourself over the head with catastrophizing, remind yourself of this essential truth and be reassured. You will save yourself needless suffering, and only you have the power to pull yourself out of such misery.

You are divinely protected as you open to love. As God shelters you, you also do your part in creating a kinder, gentler world for yourself. You are led in the best ways to protect yourself, creating a haven for your heart in which you are able to remain openhearted, a magnet for love.

7

Forget the One Hundred Frogs

The Seventh Magnet: Discover Your Own Love Style

Some of the old saws about dating make it seem so unattractive that it's a wonder we all haven't become monks and nuns, giving up on mating entirely. The conventional idea that "you have to kiss a hundred frogs to find your prince" is enough to send anyone back into a cave. Many of the limited notions floating around make dating sound like sheer drudgery. People still repeat the frog cliché back to me as though it makes sense. It doesn't. I have never found love to be a numbers game, and I don't believe that meeting your soulmate is a matter of either chance or plotting out the right course. You don't need to up the odds by

KERRY AND LARY: A LOVE STORY

Lary and Kerry were both in search of their soulmates. Each had a ritual in which they would go for coffee at the Washington Street Pier in Marina del Rey, walk out at sunset, and ask that their soulmate be sent to them. Kerry did this on Monday nights. Lary did this on Tuesday nights. One evening they found themselves together on the pier. It was sunset on a Wednesday night. They were both in search of the same thing: a partner who shared their spiritual, artistic, and intellectual interests.

Kerry was a survivor of cancer. In her fifties, she vowed that if she overcame her illness, she would live her life fully and really allow her dreams to come true.

Kerry and Lary had separately attended classes at the same spiritual center. Finally, their paths crossed at a class. Kerry noticed Lary that evening and liked his energy. The following week they happened to meet in a bookstore. Kerry had knocked over several bottles of water while reaching for one on the top shelf. Lary rushed to her side and asked if she was okay. The next night they sat across from each other at another class. They were

suffering through a million dates. There are no odds. It only takes one, the *right* one. Remember:

Nothing will keep your soulmate from you.

partners in class and exchanged phone numbers as "homework partners." The following evening they attended one of my seminars called *Manifest Your Soulmate*. Lary was just in front of Kerry in line. He turned around and said, "Well, ring ring."

They decided that meeting four times in less than two weeks was definitely a sign. They went out for a drink and Lary said, "I'm in trouble now." They found that they shared a love of spirituality and wished to live in an environment filled with "trees, hills, and water." Lary discovered that the place he had envisioned in his meditations for ten years was in fact the view from the living room of Kerry's vacation home in Bellingham, Washington. Kerry realized that a vision of her soulmate that her friend Shila had experienced years earlier matched Lary's appearance and his habit of underlining books.

Both Kerry and Lary came to realize that they had been heading toward each other for many years. Their desires, their visions, and their hearts had been yearning for the other. I had the honor of marrying them in a beautiful seaside ceremony, appropriately, at sunset.

You don't have to kiss one single person that you don't want to kiss. Not one. What an unappetizing notion—to kiss someone you're not attracted to! If you are seeing someone who you have no interest in kissing or getting physically close to, this is a sign that he is not your One. In this instance it is best to release this person or officially turn the relationship into a friendship and move on.

Another outdated idea that most experts can't even believe I disagree with is "You have to get yourself 'out there' in order to find love. You won't meet him sitting at home and twiddling your thumbs." As a matter of fact, you very well could.

HE'LL HAVE A WRECK IN YOUR YARD

One of my stock "Southernisms" always gets a laugh in my workshops:

> If you are not the going-out type, he'll have a wreck in your yard.

The fact is that when I first began saying this, I had ample evidence that it was true—countless stories of people who actually met their love while *staying home*. After a few years of teaching this truth, I now have stories upon stories of lovers who met in one of their homes, and the file keeps growing. Here are some real-life examples of people who met their One while staying home:

- Deb, a tailor, met Wally when he came to her home to have some altering done. They have now been happily married for many years.
- Victoria and Michael were neighbors. She lived upstairs, he down. Victoria was actively dating, trying to find her One. Meanwhile, Michael noticed

her being picked up on dates and wished someday he would be her date. Close proximity worked its magic, and they eventually began dating. Now the two are married with a child. It turns out that the best thing for Victoria's love life was staying home.

- James met Barb while on his computer at home, through online dating. When they met in person, he knew quickly that she was his soulmate. They soon bought a house together and are now engaged.
- Mike came to install some new electronics in Daphne's house and was instantly smitten with her. Over the course of hours he worked in her house, they bonded and eventually she invited him to stay for dinner. For the next year, they never spent a night apart. The two are now engaged and planning their destination wedding.

What these examples illustrate is that it is not necessary to force yourself to get out if this is not your style. Homebodies still manage to find love. If you are doing the inner work to open up to your love, he very well may come to you. Or you will run into each other. That is why it's so important to send out the soul call that you learned about in chapter 2. Your soul call does the work for you, so you don't have to struggle through the difficult process of looking for love.

The reasons for this are many:

- First, if you are not the type to hang out at bars, for example, why force yourself to go to a bar? It's doubtful that anyone who is compatible with you will be there, since most of the people are in the place because they like bars. It makes more sense to do things you like to do, even if it's being a homebody.

- Second, I've mentioned that the inner work you do is much more critical to magnetizing your love than anything you do in the way of outer work. If you're doing the inner work and stay open, love will literally land on your doorstep.
- Third, love is a natural, spontaneous phenomenon, and I've rarely seen it happen in any sort of planned way. Love is not something you can methodically plot to get. Logic fails in this arena. It is only too common for people I've worked with to do backflips in an attempt to bring on love, only to fail. When they quit working so hard at getting love, that's when the magic happened.

All of these bring to mind a common question I often get:

"I feel like I need to attend every event that's happening. What if she's at the one event that I skip? I'm petrified that I'll somehow miss her. What should I do?"

My answer is: "Relax."

YOU COULD MEET YOUR SOULMATE ANYWHERE AT ANY TIME

If the Universe has determined that you need to be in a particular place in order to run into your One, you will be led to the perfect place at the right time. It bears repeating:

> You can't miss your soulmate.

It's as though you both have been implanted with homing devices that magnetize you to each other. And if you don't get the chance to connect at first, you'll be thrown together again and again until it finally "takes."

Londin and Jake spied each other at a seminar. Jake was on a panel of men speaking on the subject of "understanding men," and Londin was in the audience. Since Jake was on the stage, it was natural for Londin to notice him, but what is amazing is that Jake noticed her out of all the women in the audience. Not only that, but he managed to read her name tag from the stage, and didn't forget her name for the next two years. When a friend of his wanted to set him up with a certain woman, his ears perked up when he heard her name was Londin. The mutual friend gave Jake her phone number, but he was too scared to call. Londin remembered Jake from the seminar and told the friend she would love to hear from him. Jake finally did call, and the rest is history. They fell madly in love and are now married, planning a family.

Danny and Cameron, who met at a mutual friend's party, are another couple who were thrown together repeatedly until it was right. The first time she saw Danny, Cameron was with her then-boyfriend and should not have been noticing Danny, but she did. Danny noticed her, too. Over the next four years, they saw each other occasionally through the mutual friend, but one or the other was involved in a relationship. Finally, both were single at the same moment, and it didn't take long for them to hook up. It was a relief when they came together, because the tension between the two had built up over the years.

You can't miss your soulmate. All that is needed is trust in timing, trust in the process, and openness to inner guidance. As the above examples illustrate, you will be thrown together until the time is right. You can expedite this process by continuing to do your inner work, such as self-esteem boosting, releasing past relationships and negative thoughts, and keeping your spirits high.

BACKFLIPS NOT NECESSARY

You never need to do something that is counter to your being in order to obtain love. If you dislike dating, you need never go on another date. I've had many clients who dated only their soulmate in the process of opening to love. There are even more who never kissed anyone until they were in the arms of their One. Unless you enjoy kissing lots of different people, you can safely discard the notion of kissing one hundred frogs to find your prince. I believe that opening to your love can be easy, fun, and not the least bit uncomfortable. In fact, it is quite exciting! Affirm this for yourself, and release any beliefs you have about needing to do things that make you uncomfortable to find love.

AN EXCEPTION: WHEN KISSING A HUNDRED FROGS IS A GOOD THING

Every now and then there's someone in one of my workshops who *needs* to date and date lots of people. Sometimes they know this, and sometimes they become gradually aware of how beneficial dating is for them. These are usually people who have something to heal, and their method of healing is by dating a great deal. Who are these people? Often they are people who were wallflowers or very shy in high school or college, who need to understand that they are attractive to the opposite sex after all. Sometimes they are people who need to experience a lot of dating in order to learn to relate better to the opposite sex. These are but a few of the examples of those for whom kissing a hundred frogs is beneficial.

If you know someone who is going through a phase of dating around, don't judge him. Understand that this is part of his process and be supportive. And if you are one of these people, accept it and revel in it (while making sure you're honest with each date that you are playing the field). Ask for your friends' support and understanding as you enjoy this part of your life. Eventually, you will be delivered into the arms of your soulmate with a lot of fond memories and a part of yourself healed.

BOBBY'S COMPUTER

Bobby had been single and lonely for a while. One day, he got a new computer. After spending hours putting it together and trying to understand how it worked, he finally managed to open the word processing program. Frustrated from his labors and feeling his loneliness more than usual, Bobby managed to type five words.

I demand my soulmate now.

Then, ready for a break, he grabbed a jacket and hurried out the door to a pool joint around the corner from his house. Ordering a beer, he noticed an attractive woman looking at a pool table. He asked her if she wanted to play, and she said yes, introducing herself. Bobby and Kim played several games of pool and bonded in the process. Soon they were inseparable. After that, everyone wanted to use Bobby's "lucky" computer. Moral of the story: when you get bold enough to demand something from the Universe, that energy has real strength and your demand is met. Affirm for yourself that you will get what you want.

♥ MAGNETIZATION STEP 7 ♥
GET IN TOUCH WITH YOUR LOVE STYLE

As you have been reading this chapter, you probably noticed that I negated some of your beliefs about finding love. Had you resigned yourself to kissing a hundred frogs before finding love? Did you buy the concept that you had to get "out there"? Have you actually done some things you didn't want to do in your quest for love, such as kissing someone you didn't want to kiss, or forcing yourself to join an online dating service even though it isn't your style?

In your Soulmate Journal make a list of anything you don't like about dating, personal beliefs or actions that made you cringe when it comes to love, and anything that is not comfortable for you (going to a bar, speed dating, getting fixed up, forcing yourself to go out when you'd rather stay home). Answer this question: "What thought prompted you to force yourself to do something that was distasteful to you?" Write down what thoughts you've had about love that make you squeamish. If the word "dating" strikes terror in your heart, then clearly you have some negative beliefs about finding love. Write down all of these ideas so that you can determine what has given you this dread.

After you have made your list, put your hand on the list and say out loud: "None of these things are true for me and my love life. I never have to do anything I don't want to in pursuit of love. My love will come to me in a way that is fun and easy for us both."

Now take some moments to think about the ways it would be fun for you to meet your love. If you are a real homebody or even homebound, it's fine to imagine that your love will show up at your door. This has happened for other people, so why not for you? Once you get an image of ways that would be natural for you to connect with your soulmate, record your thoughts in your Soulmate Journal.

Clip pictures from magazines that remind you of ways you can envision meeting your One.

If you find yourself falling back into limited thinking about how love can come to you, reread this chapter and go over the notes in your journal to remind yourself that you will obtain love your own way, in a manner that fits your unique love style.

I affirm that love lands right in your lap. Because you have been doing the inner work, forces are coming to your aid to engineer your union with your soulmate. I release any fear you have that you will have to settle or kiss anyone you don't want to. You can rest in the faith that love is on its way.

8

The Mating Dance

The Eighth Magnet: Date in a Completely Different Manner

In one of my workshops, a woman named Susan raised her hand to ask this question: "I seem to always attract unavailable guys. What am I doing wrong?" When I asked her if she ever had guys interested in her whom she didn't find attractive, she said, "Yes, but they don't count, because I'm not interested."

"So what you're telling me is that sometimes you are attracted to guys who are not available to you. And other times you're pursued by men to whom *you're* not available, because you're not attracted to them. Maybe those men don't count to you, but it does happen."

"Well, yes, I guess," Susan replied.

My next observation surprised Susan and everyone else in the workshop.

"This sounds like normal dating to me. You would not be here if things had worked out yet in your love life. If so, you'd be with your boyfriend or husband, not needing this workshop, right?"

"True," she said.

"Expect it to be just like this until your soulmate comes along. It's what dating *looks like!*" I pointed out. "Either you like the guy more, he likes you more, or it's just not 'clicking.' I rarely meet someone who is dating who has a pattern that's different. Once you're with your soulmate, you won't be dating anymore. He'll be ready to go the whole nine yards with you, and you'll be crazy for him. You'll quickly go beyond the dating phase. But until he takes you off the market for good, this is the stage you're in. Don't expect it to be different until you meet your soulmate."

"But how do I break this pattern of dating guys who are unavailable?" she asked. Susan was not going to let go of this one easily.

"You don't have to," I said. "It doesn't sound real to me, seeing as how you also meet men who you're not available to. And even if it were a true pattern and not just a distorted perception, the minute your One shows up, the pattern will evaporate instantaneously. There is no way that you'll miss your soulmate, and no possibility that he'll be unavailable. Whatever you've been experiencing in general will not apply to this one person, your true love."

I can't tell you how many times I've heard variations of Susan's question. One man, Ken, wanted to know why every woman he met said he was a great friend but there wasn't any chemistry. If I'd been a traditional love consultant, I would have asked him to change himself in some way. And boy, did Ken ever want me to give him a solution like that! But I couldn't. I believed that if Ken had tried to become something he's not, he would have missed his soulmate. How would she recognize him if he was busy acting a part rather than being himself? It doesn't matter if fifty women found him to be great friendship material but lacking in sex appeal. This would never mean there is something wrong with Ken, that he is somehow unattractive or wimpy, all of which he was afraid were true. I knew that the minute his soulmate came along, they would have the crackling chemistry that soulmates share.

Unlike what many dating experts may say, dating is not a numbers game. It doesn't matter if fifty people are attracted to you or just one (and there will always be one: the right One). You don't need to try to attract droves of men or women. This would be an ego exercise. Though some people may attempt changing themselves in an effort to shore up their insecurities, such insincerity is not in sync with personal integrity. It may even scare off a soulmate (at least temporarily). Ken's work was to believe in himself, and to understand that just because he was gifted at having friendships with women didn't mean he was unequipped for love.

Ken struggled with his feelings for a long time, but eventually improved his self-image. We worked on learning to see himself in a more favorable light, releasing past bad love experiences, and truly understanding what a catch he was, all while keeping his heart open and hopes high. I was pleased that he never gave in to the urge to try to make himself over. Instead, he did the inner work to accept that he is fine the way he is. Shortly, Heather showed up, and she thought Ken was the sexiest man she'd ever met. Heather was a strong woman, who was turned off by macho men. The two couldn't see past each other, and are now in love. They enjoy a passionate love life together. If you were now to ask Ken if he still thinks he's lacking anything, he would probably say, "Huh?" like you're crazy and then run off to kiss Heather. All of his struggles with this issue are forgotten. He is too busy reveling in this newfound love. The best part is that in addition to their passion for each other, Ken and Heather are best friends. All of the friendship practice with other women helped Ken to enter a rich relationship on every level.

Everything happens for a reason.

Have faith that you are perfect for your soulmate. There are no patterns you have that will prevent him or her from finding you and recognizing you as the One. Yes, you may have issues to resolve inside of yourself, spiritual growth to do. But you are a perfect being, and there is nothing wrong with you, no matter what anyone may tell you or how you may feel if someone has rejected you.

BUT I HATE TO DATE

People tell me quite often that they hate dating. I understand. Our current model of dating—dinner, a movie, stilted conversation—is an awkward mating ritual. My idea of dating is broader. I define dating as anything you do to get to know a prospective romantic partner. It may look like going to work and flirting at the water cooler. Perhaps it's connecting at a weekend retreat. Maybe you hang out with your best friend until you and her brother fall in love. Whatever it looks like in this getting-to-know-you phase, an emotional bond is being created. If you haven't done any traditional courting, it is wise to acknowledge in a formal way your mutual attraction. Taking a woman out to dinner, bringing her flowers, picking her up when you have plans together are ways of honoring her, letting her know you think she's special. Even if you didn't start out dating traditionally, it's wise to pay homage to traditional romantic gestures or at least romance in general. You don't necessarily have to be traditional as long as you make sure you're respecting each other's needs to be courted in some fashion.

There is no skipping this process called dating. It is one of the stages toward walking hand in hand with your beloved. You may never go on a traditional date with anyone but your One. But the fact is that even then you must do the getting-to-know-you dance with your soulmate. There are steps you can take to make this process more tolerable, even fun. The first step is to be willing to dive into dating and surrender any preconceived notions about how it has to look. The second step is to take every opportunity to understand your new love, listening to childhood stories, past hurts, and dreams for the future. A good third step is to become aware of her emotional patterns. We all handle situations differently; you should begin to notice how she copes with stress, confrontation, loving moments, and even good-byes. What you do together takes a back seat to this process of connection and intimacy. The fourth step is to introduce her to your world and ask to be shown her world as well: friends, interests, family, favorite haunts, work environment. Once you're willing, you can begin opening up to something that turns out to be a delicious time in your life. This phase can be one that you always look back on fondly. When the two of you are in your rocking chairs, watching your grandchildren playing in the yard, you can share fond memories of the courting phase of your relationship.

RELEASE YOUR PICTURE OF DATING

Be receptive to alternative ways of dating. To do this, you must surrender any rigid ideas of how dating has to look. Love comes in many forms, and the more open you are, the quicker you'll find it. Vow that from here on you will adjust your thoughts on dating to embrace this fun stage of your journey to love.

I'VE BEEN ALONE FOR YEARS—WHAT DO I DO?

When you haven't been in a relationship for a long time, it may be because you have put up walls to love without even realizing it. You may have even developed an idea that you are so set in your ways that you couldn't possibly integrate someone into your life. The thought of sharing your life with someone or living together may sound impossible. The good news is that you can change this.

First, do the inner work to open to love. You can do this by:

- Sending out a soul call as you did in chapter 2.
- Figuratively and literally making space in your life for someone new (also discussed in chapter 2).
- Releasing any old relationships you've been hanging on to, which you should have done in chapter 5.
- Emotionally healing any old hurts so that you don't put walls up against love. Be willing to get beyond any bitterness or wounds from the past so that you can be open. We talk about this in chapter 5, and you may need to keep on working at it. It can be a challenging process.

Now it's time to do some outer work. Start dating or at least connecting with possible love interests. This is to make sure your sexual energy is open. I work with countless people who are shut down in that regard. This is all well and good, quite proper, but with your soulmate, of course, you want to be open to him or her sexually. Flirting is a way to open your sexual energy in a light, fun way. If you have suppressed your flirtatious side, it's time to let it come out and play. Everyone has their own style of flirting. For some people, it's with a look. For others, it's with light patter. Other flirting styles may include touch, body language, tone of voice, or even showing off (this is common in adolescent boys).

This notion of having to flirt scares many people in my workshops. But what they don't realize is not only that

THE OPENER

Penelope hadn't dated in years and was celibate for longer than she cared to remember. She met Joel at a festival. They connected, but she was too shy at the time to allow a serious relationship to happen. He lived in another town, but they kept in touch after their first meeting. He announced his intention to come visit her for her birthday, and she agreed to the trip, albeit with mixed emotions. When she picked him up from the airport, she was a nervous wreck. They then went to lunch. This gave them time to feel their way into each other and get used to being in each other's presence again. This is often necessary when you haven't been on a date in a while. When the couple got back to Penelope's house, Joel attempted to get close to her. She confessed to him her nervousness, and even cried. He took her into his arms and reassured her that there was no pressure and that she could take her time in getting comfortable with his presence.

During Joel's visit, the two gradually got closer physically and emotionally. Penelope was smitten. However, Joel told her at one point that he wasn't sure she was his soulmate, so she was

flirting is an essential ingredient in mating rituals in every culture, but also that they have probably done it in past relationships without realizing they were flirting. Flirting is instinctual. If you have ever dated anyone, ever been in love, you probably sent out some signals of interest without even conflicted. Meanwhile, one night while sleeping in Joel's arms, she had a dream about someone else. He was gentle like Joel, but bigger and blonder. When she awoke the next morning, she was confused. Why was she so into this man next to her but having dreams of someone else? She tearfully told Joel goodbye when he left, and they made plans to meet each other the next month at a large gathering.

Penelope traveled to the gathering with a bunch of friends, including Jerry, a man she had always found attractive. The two connected during the trip, flirting, and by the end of the drive Penelope was in Jerry's lap as they drove through the grounds of the gathering site. She was conflicted about Joel, but remembered him saying that he didn't think she was his soulmate. For this reason and others, such as the dream she had, Penelope chose Jerry over Joel, though it wasn't easy telling Joel about her change of heart. Penelope and Jerry's romance quickly heated up. Now she is married to Jerry with several children. Penelope believes that the man she dreamed of while in Joel's arms is Jerry. He is gentle like Joel, but taller and blonder, just like in the dream.

knowing it. A good exercise to get in touch with your "inner flirt" is to look to your past for how you acted when you were interested in someone or starting a relationship. You can also try some of the following techniques to see how they work for you:

- Make eye contact with people you find attractive. Sustain the eye contact for a moment or two and then look away. Perhaps look again.
- Open your body posture by uncrossing your arms and legs. Arch your back and put your palms out when talking to someone of interest.
- Try touching someone you are drawn to. While in conversation, lightly touch her arm to make a point. If your rapport progresses, you can even try rubbing her back and see what the response is.
- Practice making your voice "flirty." If that seems difficult or uncomfortable, pretend you're Mae West or Pepé Le Pew and have some fun getting used to what your voice sounds like when you want to be inviting.

Sometimes people who haven't had a romantic relationship in years rely on an "opener." An opener is someone who comes along and helps you get back into the groove of being in a relationship again. This is someone you date, and often get sexually involved with. It can be a satisfying relationship but without the deep soul connection you will have with your One. Your opener will not be your soulmate, but you can be eternally grateful to him for being the connection that helped you to release any barriers you've had to love.

How do you know if the person you finally get involved with after all of this time is your soulmate or just an opener? As the relationship progresses, you will be able to tell.

DESPERATION REPELS

Have you ever noticed how needy people can be scary? You may find yourself making excuses to avoid them. Desperation and dating don't mix. Too many singles functions have an air of anxiety clouding them. Everyone has expectations. One man told me he felt like he was "putting himself on the line" by going to a singles dance, and he was uncomfortable. Avoiding any place that feels awkward is not a bad idea. An even better idea is to avoid feeling desperate yourself.

> *Don't let yourself get desperate. Instead, know that you don't have to feel needy, even if you can't quite see how or when your soulmate will appear. You can afford to be choosy, and you are "hot," especially to your soulmate. Act like it.*

SIGNS THAT YOU ARE ACTING/FEELING DESPERATE

- You find yourself trying too hard when you're around someone who is attractive to you.
- You feel like a wallflower at a party or event.
- Fearing that you'll miss out on love, you force yourself to approach every person you are attracted to and go to every event where there will be single people.
- You're off-balance, feeling neither secure nor attractive.

Making sure you feel confident about love is important. The single most attractive trait cited by both women and men is confidence. There is no reason you shouldn't feel good about yourself and your prospects for love. Even if you're certain that you're not God's gift to the opposite sex, you are the best thing that ever happened to your soulmate. Hold that thought as you open yourself to exploring romance. The whole dance becomes easier when you know what the end result will be.

One benefit of not being desperate is that you won't try to make the wrong person fit. People who are desperate try to squeeze someone who is inappropriate into the role of mate. This never works out, and is a contributing factor to many breakups. If less pressure were felt, and people walked through their single days with patience and confidence, more people would be with their soulmates. Because you know love is on its way, the whole process of getting there can be explored without rushing. It can even be enjoyed. Do whatever you can to feel attractive and eradicate desperation from your being. The energy of desperation is not worth your time, and it could hinder your soulmate from arriving. It only takes one person for you, the right One. You can afford to be choosy, since you know that your One is on the way.

♥ MAGNETIZATION STEP 8 ♥
MAKE DATING BEARABLE, EVEN FUN

In your Soulmate Journal, write down your best and worst dating experiences. What was the easiest coming-together with a mate that you've had so far? As you read the following section, make a list of the biggest mistakes you have made in dating (i.e., bad communication, having an agenda, taking things personally, not being honest). Leave space after each entry. Additionally, go back to each item and write down how you can correct those mistakes, using suggestions that I make (i.e., drop my agenda, listen better, quit taking wrong fits as rejection, learn to say no better). Also make notes of dating techniques you'd like to try that may make the mating dance a whole different world for you.

Below are ways you can enhance the dating experience for yourself. We've discussed the first steps, which are:

- Having a rock-solid faith that your soulmate is out there and that you can't miss him.
- Feeling confident and not desperate.

Next, look at the whole experience of dating differently. Let's start with the person you are on a date with. Whoever she is, the bottom line is that she's another human being. Maybe she's not perfect and you find yourself not particularly attracted to her, but she is a human and therefore inherently interesting. If you find a person boring, you're not looking deep enough. Once you understand that you don't have to make anything fit, you can relax and enjoy your time exploring this person. As mentioned, you don't have to even kiss if it feels wrong. There is a school of thought that says every encounter you have with another person is holy. This thinking works well in dating. You never know what gift your date might have for you. Maybe she's the One and you simply don't yet recognize her as such. At least ten stories come to mind of couples who were convinced their spouse wasn't "it" on the first date. Gradually, their beloved grew on them until they found themselves madly in love.

I've also heard many stories involving a date who became the vehicle through which the soulmate was introduced (best friend, sister, coworker, you name it). Be open. You never know what forces may be at work. At this point, you've done the inner work to call forth your soulmate. Now trust the process as it unfolds.

Drop Your Agenda

Drop your agenda for your date. It has been said that a woman wears her wedding dress on the first date while the man is busy trying to get her in bed. Both of these are agendas. If you're on a blind date and it's not going well, your agenda may be to end the date as soon as possible. Any agenda gets in the way of the process. It is dishonoring of the other person. Become willing just to *be* with the other person. Spending time with that person is an exercise in living fully in the now, enjoying what is before you with no pressure. Revel in the moment. You never know what gift it may bring.

How can you drop your agenda? It requires your being present in each moment of your time together. You can ask questions about your date to engage better and pay attention to the answers. Pretending that later you'll be quizzed on facts about your date will force you to be attentive. Also be willing to share some of yourself. Tell stories, reveal what you've been up to lately, and make every effort to find the common ground between the two of you. There is always something that you will find you share.

Remember There Is No Rejection

I have gone over this earlier, but it bears mentioning again as you step out and date. The concept of getting dumped is not real. I've never seen it to be true. As I have dealt with people who are supposedly the dumper and the dumpee, inevitably the situation has been more complicated than that. Both had torn feelings, and often, the person who was the supposed dumper actually felt like he was the dumpee. Things are never so clear-cut, but above all, rejection is not what is happening. It is a matter of a wrong fit, an incompatibility. If your date is not your soulmate, it simply won't work out, and if you're not strong enough to walk away, the door will be shut for you. Knowing there is no rejection makes it much easier to date.

To Quit Feeling Awkward, Focus on the Other Person

Many people find themselves self-conscious on dates, worrying about whether they'll make a good impression. This approach is wrongheaded. We've talked about self-confidence and not being desperate. Let's add something else to the mix. Instead of focusing on yourself and how you're doing on the date, you are better served by giving your date attention. Work on connecting with him. Each date is an opportunity to work on your listening skills. The greatest personality in the world can't compete with a skilled listener. Listening is the best way to relate with someone else. It is an ability that can serve you well in many arenas. Look into your date's eyes deeply. Some people avoid much eye contact, but looking into someone's eyes creates a powerful connection. Hang on to every word that comes from your

FIVE WAYS TO BREAK YOUR BAD DATING PATTERNS

Many people tell me they have a dating pattern that they hate. Perhaps they're always attracted to unavailable types. Or they habitually fall in love with someone who will abandon them abruptly after a period of time. Or they find addictive personalities highly attractive. And even though I'm a firm believer that once you connect with your soulmate, your pattern will spontaneously dissolve, here are some ways to change your dating pattern even before that.

1. Say no. The first step to getting what you want is saying no to what you don't want. Be brave enough to turn your back the minute you see that your unsuccessful dating pattern is coming up again.
2. If you find yourself dating someone and falling into your usual pattern, and you are unhappy, go ahead and say good-bye. Bite the bullet and go through the pain of letting go (see chapter 5) so that you can be free for something different that *will* make you happy.

date's mouth, and do so with your whole body. Suspend any judgment you may feel, and don't interrupt with a related story of your own. Ask questions to bring your date out. Remind yourself that you don't have to marry this person or go out on another date, but for now you will be fully *with* your date, completely present and willing to connect.

3. Don't let yourself feel desperate. When we are feeling desperate, we tend to settle for less than what we want. You are *not* desperate. Better to be alone than date the same old, same old. Go forward in faith that you will get what you want.
4. Try something new. It may feel weird at first to date someone who is different than your usual type, but it's a good thing. You will get used to it. You may just not be accustomed to something that is actually healthy for you.
5. Pray, meditate, do affirmations, and read uplifting words. These spiritual tools will help you stay in a good place *and* introduce grace into your life. Miracles will abound!

I affirm for you that even as you are reading this, your old, unsatisfying patterns are going out the window, and it's a new day for you!

There are eight different levels of communication, which will be discussed in chapter 10. The lowest forms are violence and, up a couple of notches, arguing. Even debating is a low form of communicating. Try not to argue with your date about anything, even if you have strong opinions. You can get into issues later, if you do have a strong opinion. This is not to stifle being yourself, but instead to keep the energy on a positive note until you know each other better and have had a chance to create an emotional bond. If you two are not compatible, don't make another date, but avoid getting into a debate. Instead, go for the higher levels of communication—conversing, relating, and communion (which can be anything from reading each other's minds to transcendent electric sex—something you will definitely have with your soulmate!).

As you connect with your date, this bond helps you to forget any butterflies in your stomach. When you're engaged in the present, it takes you beyond self-consciousness. You're too busy listening to worry about how you're coming across. And it keeps you in the moment. You can't "futurize"—whether it's getting her in the sack or naming your first child. Futurizing takes away from the fun to be had in the here and now.

Quit Sweating Every Phone Call

The concept of a make-or-break moment is a false one. Rarely does a relationship that's growing hinge on one phone call or misstep. It doesn't work that way. Women and men can drive themselves crazy when they're dating by sweating each conversation, each phone call, each gesture.

It may be a stereotype, but it has been known to be true that some women wait by the phone and agonize if he doesn't call in two days. (Note to women: it is said that five women days equal one guy day. This should help you feel less anxious when it takes him what you deem a "long time" to call.) Guys, on the other hand, beat themselves up if they feel they didn't take her to the right restaurant.

To calm yourself, keep in mind that the low-level anxiety that can occur with dating is simply your innate fears coming up. Dating is a time when you are opening your heart, making yourself vulnerable, and it can be nerve-wracking. Recognize this as a time to nurture yourself and to grow more confident about who you are. Understand that many people would consider you a great catch, and that there is no doubt you will take your soulmate's breath away.

At times during the dating process, you may attract someone who reflects your worst judgments about yourself. Worry about your derriere, and he'll tell you that if you lost ten pounds off the back end, you'd be perfect. Worry you're not successful enough for her, and the next thing you know, she'll express skepticism about your abilities as a provider.

Be aware that we each have a magnetic field around us, specific to our own self-doubts. At times we will actually draw someone to us who mirrors back our fears and insecurities. It is tempting to indulge the doubter, to give credence to what he says and try to change, hoping that you can win him over, but it's no use. What's coming up inside of you is not about the other person, but about your own insecurities. Address the issues within yourself, and cut the doubter loose. If this skeptic is your One, he will come back around. Most likely, he's not the one, and in releasing him you're opening yourself up to your soulmate.

One thought that will keep you going despite the insecurity is a phrase I find people need to hear repeatedly: *Nothing can keep your soulmate from you.* You need to hear this over and over for it to sink in. Your garlic breath after going out for Italian will not keep your soulmate from finding you appealing. That dumb joke you regretted the minute it was out of your mouth will not keep your soulmate from thinking your talent approaches the level of Jim Carrey. The fact that your thighs looked a little chunky in the red mini you wore on your third date will not make your soulmate any less attracted to you. Even his needing to make sure that his previous girlfriend is not really the One will not keep him from finally figuring out that you're *it* for him, and he wants you in his life for good.

You *cannot* screw it up. Making your way to your soulmate is a foolproof journey. Knowing that you and your soulmate are traveling toward each other makes the whole process of dating much easier to enjoy. She will show up for sure and will not be able to see past you.

Give Your Date a Break

You are not the only one whose insecurities are coming up. Your date will have an equal case of nerves. His own anxieties about dating, about doing things right, and about who he is will also be at play. Be as gentle with him as you are learning to be with yourself. There should be no false pressure on either one of you to make the relationship fit. Forget about any preordained timing like expectations of sex by a certain date, a commitment after dating a few months, and so forth. There are no "shoulds" in dating, and any obligation someone might feel to "put out" by the third date is ridiculous. For many people, this is too soon and adds strain to an already stressful situation.

As you put your date at ease by giving her latitude, you deepen the connection, allowing the space and freedom to see what's there and what's not. She will sense your suspension of judgment and feel secure. Bunny and Ralph's story is an excellent example of this. Bunny met Ralph at a weekend gathering. It was cold, and Bunny half-jokingly suggested Ralph come over and keep her warm all night. Surprised when he showed up at her cabin, she was impressed that he held her in his arms all night long, fully clothed, without making any sexual advances toward her. Bunny trusted Ralph after that night, and the relationship heated up. Now they are married.

Many opportunities will arise for you to be a gracious date. If you find yourself starting to react to something, rein yourself in, and choose the high road. Make light of any awkward moments. Ryan got a flat tire while on a date with Ally. Instead of moaning about it, Ally chose to find humor in the situation, and they had a laugh fest the rest of the night. They, too, ended up tying the knot. Overlook as much as you are able to. You can always opt out of future dates if you find signs that you are truly incompatible, but while you are together, do your best to make it a light, enjoyable date.

THE DRAW OF THE UNATTAINABLE

There is a certain pull of the unattainable. In general, people don't go after others who haven't shown some interest and who might "reject" them. However, if there has been some connection and yet the other person is not quite available, a strange allure can result. I've often seen people in sessions who are mildly interested in someone, only to become wildly attracted when that person pulls away. This is a version of the "rubberband effect," I talked about in chapter 5. Beware of this effect.

If the allure of someone is heightened by their unavailability, that attraction will diminish once you "get" that person. The measure of how at play the "rubberband effect" is can be how attracted you were before the other person became hard to get. This sort of magnetism is temporary. It can cloud the issue of whether your love interest is your soulmate. Be cautious about this sort of situation until you can properly sort it out.

Rob wasn't certain of his feelings for Casey and finally decided to break up with her. When he ran into Casey with her new boyfriend a few months later, he found himself more attracted to her than he had ever been while they were dating. He worked to get her back, and she finally succumbed, splitting up with her boyfriend to be with Rob. Once they were back together, Rob's attraction began to fade, and they were right back at square one. If he had been more aware of the rubber band effect, he could have avoided this situation, spared Casey needless pain, and saved himself some time and angst. They broke up again, and Rob finally learned his lesson about giving in to the allure of the unattainable.

FREEDOM: NO STRINGS

Society subtly frowns upon people who want to play the field, going out on many dates before they settle down. There is a pressure to settle down, even if it's just for serial monogamy. This pressure can get in the way of our need to explore and feel free before choosing the person who is right for us and entering into an exclusive relationship.

Men and women are not bad people if they choose to date around and avoid settling down until they are sure who their One is. A healthy stage in the mating dance is going through the kid-in-a-candy-store phase. This is a time when you realize how many attractive members of the opposite sex there are and are able to enjoy many of them. There is nothing wrong with checking out all of your options, as long as you are honest. Better to do it now, while you're free, than later, feeling trapped in a relationship that you want to leave so that you can sow your wild oats. There are no obligations in the dating process, and it's good to remember that. Your date should not feel pressured into committing to you before he's ready.

By the same token, many people in my workshops tell me they can't imagine dating more than one person at a time because "It would just feel wrong." I ask them to think of two attractive movie stars they like. What if they could date both of them at the same time? Would they? The answer is inevitably yes. What the people discover is that they were limiting themselves, thinking they couldn't attract more than one desirable person at a time. If you can't imagine dating several people at once, I invite you to expand your ideas of what is possible. It can be fun to date several people, and you may find that you've been limiting yourself. This does not mean you have to be promiscuous. You don't even have to kiss anyone (that's part of the freedom part). But give yourself permission to have fun with more than one person while you're still free. A reminder: if this idea doesn't appeal to you, it's not necessary, and you can affirm that the only person you date is your One. But for many people, dating a few people is not only freeing but also healing.

All is fair in love. A sense of obligation is a bad reason to stay in a relationship. You wouldn't want someone to stay with you simply because he felt guilty, rather than because he wanted to, would you?. By the same token, there is no need for you to feel obligated to date someone for any reason other than being drawn to him. It is kinder to cut someone loose instead of stringing them along, to be honest rather than "nice" and fake. You are allowed—even encouraged—to make choices, to date freely, and to say no to what you don't want.

Freedom is a basic spiritual principle. Even when you are with your soulmate, you don't own him or her, unlike what the lyrics of many love songs suggest ("You Belong to Me," "My Girl," "My Guy"). Marriage does not equal ownership. While you are dating, it is important to acknowledge the freedom between the two of you, and never assume any unspoken ties. The strongest bonds are made while honoring each other's freedom.

HOW IMPORTANT IS SEX?

There's a simple answer to this question: not very. Yes, of course, you'll have crackling chemistry with your soulmate, but sex and attraction are secondary to the relationship itself. Both the passion and the wonderful physical intimacy are results of the soulmate connection. I think it is important to go slowly with the sexual component of a new relationship, since this will happen naturally as you and your soulmate get closer. I suggest waiting awhile. Otherwise, sex could create false intimacy before it's warranted. Why is sex *not* important? Because it is simply one way of expressing love and feeling close, secondary to the relationship itself.

DETOURING PAST DATING BARRIERS

We all have boundaries that make us feel safe as we explore getting closer to other people. Women, in particular, tend to have physical limits around them to protect them from untimely sexual advances. When you have guys hitting on you, you put up walls to keep them at bay. When you get used to men making a move before you're ready, you learn to avoid situations that would invite unwanted aggressiveness. Men complain to me that "jerks" have made it hard on the good guys. "Women have so many walls up, I can't get through" goes the typical complaint.

My reply is: "Yes, but this is what you're up against, so you need to deal with it." It is a perfect opportunity for men to learn sensitivity. You can't go wrong by tuning in to your date at a subtle level. If you've been practicing your listening skills, you've become aware of the nonverbal cues your date gives. You can tell when she's bored or hungry. You won't miss the body language that says she's ready to go home. You'll know when she doesn't want to talk about something and be able to steer the conversation in another direction.

As you connect on a deep level, you will know when there is an opening to get closer, and you will recognize a boundary without her having to even say anything. This level of honoring and sensitivity reaps great rewards. It is practice for connecting with your soulmate and for being a more "plugged-in" person. You are opening to levels that will serve you in countless ways. She will begin to trust you and open herself to you. I call this level of communication "communion," where practical intuition takes place and words are not needed. This is a by-product of being with your soulmate. By learning to recognize unspoken boundaries and honor them, you are that much closer to true fulfillment. And who knows? Maybe this date will turn out to be your One. The rule of thumb is not to assume anything, and make each move toward her with great care.

Men, too, have their boundaries. Men's dating limits tend to be more verbal and energetic than physical. Give him a back rub or have sex, and it's no problem. But heaven forbid you bring up his last relationship or his stance on marriage and children. And don't even think of snooping in his nightstand when he's in the bathroom. One common male boundary has to do with assumptions. Until it is overtly stated, don't assume you are his girlfriend or have exclusive rights to him. Don't assume you are monogamous or that he's seeing only you. It behooves you to be as sensitive to him as you want him to be with you, even if you think his boundaries aren't as serious. Doing so is a way of honoring him, and it will open him up. Be very aware with the person you're dating. I am not saying you have to put up with anything that feels difficult or uncomfortable, but I do think it's important to honor each other's boundaries at least long enough to discern whether this is your soulmate.

The bottom line is to check in with the other person before assuming anything. You want to make sure you know where he is so that you can respect him and not make inappropriate presumptions. You can overdo the communication by hounding him every other day about where you are as a couple or how he's feeling about it. This smacks of desperation. But if your intention is to honor him and to make sure you're on the same page, it is valuable to check in with him either verbally or intuitively on a regular basis. How do you do this? Simply take some quiet time for yourself and do whatever best centers you. For many, prayer and meditation are effective tools for this. Once you feel relaxed, you can ask your intuition to speak to you about this relationship. Examine your date's behaviors, what you are feeling about your relating, and any other clues you have to determine what is going on with the two of you. Since bringing up the status of the relationship to your date too often can be annoying or can even drive him away, checking in intuitively is an alternative way to ascertain where the relationship stands at a given time.

TAKE THE HIGH ROAD

For some reason, harsh language when you're talking about your dating life is socially acceptable. People use it as a defense against feeling vulnerable. They plug up their fears by reducing the interaction of dating to the lowest common denominator. Phrases used in this coarse realm are:

Dumping: breaking up.

Getting some, do her, how good was she?: sexual references.

A dog: unattractive woman or man.

Armpiece, mercy date, gold digger, too good for him: date labels to peg a person as a less than perfect partner.

These are just a few examples of a realm that you should try to avoid. It is a low, petty way to look at people and dating. Not only is this kind of talk not honorable, but it also lowers you to a level that is not good for you. Labels do not hold up and are not accurate. No one can be reduced to a label. The sacredness of each interaction is to be acknowledged, and the vulnerability inherent in exploring a connection should be honored. Each opening that someone offers you should be cherished for what it is, even if you are not interested in the person romantically. As we have discussed, there is no such thing as rejection, only the wrong fit. Keep reminding yourself of this so that you don't take someone else's words or actions personally. If your date tells you she is not attracted to you, there is no need to feel offended and unattractive. Instead, try to understand the truth: the two of you are not right for each other. You don't have to denigrate her to your friends or insult her to her face. And you don't have to let it make you feel unappealing. Take the high road. The rewards for doing so are many. You will feel better about yourself and will learn deeper levels of respect for the other person.

WHEN YOU'RE NOT FEELING A CONNECTION

Q: Is having trouble saying no a gender issue? Do both women and men exhibit an inability to be direct?

A: I've seen both genders have this problem equally. Neither seems to have an easy time of being direct.

Q: When there seems to be no connection between two people, are men more likely to avoid giving women the bad news, or are women equally guilty of avoiding potential conflict?

A: Men and women are equally to blame. Women don't want to have to say they have no interest any more than guys do. Both sexes develop pretty elaborate avoidance techniques that just perpetuate the problem. Guys get a worse rap for this, but unjustifiably so.

Q: Why are people turned off after one date?

A: They haven't emotionally bonded with the person yet, so it's easy to make one characteristic into a big deal and become repelled. Some skittish singles even look for an excuse not to like their date.

Q: Is that fair?

A: No! It's not fair. As mentioned earlier, studies have shown that love or attraction at first sight is fairly rare, occurring in fewer than 10 percent of all relationships.[8]

Most people have walls up against love, and it takes time for their walls to come down. Emotionally bonding happens gradually, over a period of time; therefore, it's not fair to write someone off so quickly. I think it's imperative to give a date a chance, and more than one date is necessary to really determine if there is potential for a successful relationship.

Q: When dating, should you give it another chance before you give up on him or her?

A: What have you got to lose? Strive for a real connection, and try to suspend judgment until you've both spent enough time together to feel comfortable with each other. Only then can you judge the situation.

Q: How many dates should you go on with someone to get to know them?

A: Three or four at least. This is the minimum needed to break the ice and see the possibilities.

Q: How can we keep from saying yes when we really mean no?

A: When you have given a potential connection a proper chance, and you're clear that this person is not for you, resolve that you will tell the truth. Understanding that this is the most merciful choice for all concerned makes being blunt easier. The book *He's Just Not That Into You* would not have to be written if people were honest with each other.

If you have a hard time saying no, learning to do so can be uncomfortable. So if you feel uncomfortable or like a heel when you're being honest, that's a good sign. Once you resolve that you will let the person know you're not interested, you can write out a script for yourself and even practice saying no. Because you haven't said no enough in your life, you need to get used to it. Set up a time to talk on the phone or in person (Internet, voice mail, or letter breakups are not very kind), and you can make it short and to the point.

The best course of action in saying no is simply to say, "I'm not feeling the chemistry." Everyone understands this, and there can be no argument against it. Don't get into a discussion about it, as this will make it worse for both you and him, and there is no point in talking about how you feel. The other person may want to know what he did wrong, and the worst thing you can do is get into a discussion about this. It will be hurtful and will deplete you emotionally. Repeat the fact that you feel no chemistry and then give the person a compliment such as, "You are a wonderful guy, and I'm sure the right person will feel extremely lucky to have found you." Then you can end the conversation.

Afterward you will probably feel horrible, but remember that you just broke new ground, and it will serve you for the rest of your life. Eventually, you will get used to saying no and will no longer have to go to elaborate lengths to avoid people or situations. You will be free!

NO RULES

Other than the basics outlined above, there really are no other rules about dating. Dating can look many different ways. Popular concepts of do's and don'ts simply do not hold up. Take *The Rules*, a best-selling book that rigidly prescribes behavior for women on dates. This book does have some truth in it, or it wouldn't have been so popular. The good part about it is that it models a way of behaving for women who would otherwise act desperately and not honor themselves. The bad part is that The Rules just don't work. One of the country's most prominent anthropologists, Helen E. Fisher, found in her research that women "generally initiate the courting sequence with subtle nonverbal cues."[9] If you were a "Rules girl," you wouldn't be giving any signals at all!

Lucy was as far from a "Rules girl" as you can get. In college she had a crush on Mike and was not shy about letting him know of her interest. She went so far as to follow Mike on dates with other girls, crouched in the back of a car after talking her roommate into driving. It could be construed as stalking, but Lucy's intuition told her that he was the One and open to her. Eventually, Mike succumbed to Lucy's passion for him. Mike even proposed, something that was not supposed to happen, according to The Rules. Lucy upended The Rules and still got her man. This is not behavior you would want to emulate, but it definitely illustrates the fact that there are no formulas for how love has to happen.

This is the problem with any prescription for dating. For every rule, you find an exception. There are no limits in love, so no formula will work every time. Why is this true?

Because it allows you to be *you* without worrying if you're doing things just right. There are no rules for how you need to be you. And there is no prescription for how and when you will fall in love. It all happens naturally and spontaneously. There is no right or wrong way to date. There is just *your* way. For your soulmate, it will be the perfect way.

MISMATCHED COUPLES

I recently participated in a media interview on the subject of supposed "mismatched couples," something I don't believe in. The definition of mismatches seems to be those couples who don't fit well according to societal standards. Here are some of the factors that can translate into a perceived mismatch:

- She's taller than he is.
- One's status is perceived by some as much higher than the other's—socially, economically, or simply with regard to being an insider in a group or not.
- They're from wildly different backgrounds, cultures, or religions.
- They have different ways of being, i.e., she's a conservative Southern debutante and he's in a rock band.

If you tend to date exactly who you are expected to date according to societal norms or your own inner rules, meaning you don't give potential mismatches a chance, this situation deserves a closer look. You may be too narrow-minded. And for heaven's sake, if you're perfectly content with someone who everyone else believes is a mismatch for you, ignore their opinions and go for it. (Of course, this doesn't apply to someone who is physically or verbally abusive to you or someone close to you.) There are no limits in love, and certainly not in terms of how supposedly good a match you are. If you two get married, forbid friends and family from ever mentioning your "mismatch" again.

Your soulmate is perfect for you regardless of any societal perception or mismatch. This is a bogus concept, one perpetuated by a society that attempts to quantify the unquantifiable. And by all means, refuse to put up your own fences by labeling yourself unworthy or a mismatched partner due to economic status, education, or any other factor. Otherwise, you are adding to your own worst notions about yourself and closing yourself to the gifts that the Universe has for you.

FORGET LOGIC

The concept of mismatches brings me to another valuable point about dating: *love is simply not regulated by logic and never will be.* If you've ever tried to set up two friends on a date who should be perfect for each other, you know this. Love is mysterious, defies reason, and is not regulated by our brains. It is heart-directed. In fact, the part of your brain that makes rational decisions shuts down as you fall in love. This could be scary except that you are in the hands of a Higher Power that will not steer you wrong.

But this point is good to remember as you date. Don't even bother applying logic to dating situations. Don't ever ask the question "Why didn't you love me?" or anything else that asks for logic in reference to feelings. There is no reason in the arena of love. If you spend hours agonizing over what you did wrong, why it didn't work out, or how you could now make it work, you are wasting your time. Love is to be accepted. If it doesn't work out, simply accept the fact and move on by using the release techniques described in chapter 5. Many people use the releasing ritual as a dating tool for when they become overly attached and the dating leads nowhere. If you spend time hating someone for not loving you or for no longer loving you, you are wasting valuable emotional energy. Remember that love is not guided by any analytical process, so it is futile to squander your time trying to make sense of it.

When you hook up with your soulmate, logic will not apply in the most delightful way. You can make stupid mistakes that should have screwed it up, but they won't. You can look hideous in the morning, and he will think you are the most beautiful creature he's ever encountered. The no-logic aspect of love will suddenly be a wonderful force in your favor.

DATING LATER IN LIFE

A common question I hear in my workshops is: *Is dating different when you're older?*

In my workshops I've worked with people in their teens up into their seventies. From what I've observed, dating is essentially the same no matter how old you are. You still have to get to know another being, and you still act as giddy as a teen when you first fall in love, no matter how old you are.

However, there are a couple of differences I've observed. They are as follows:

- *It feels more awkward to admit you are attracted to someone when you're older.* Teens and twenty-somethings are used to the mating dance. They do it often and are not shy about actively seeking and attracting love. Their pool of possible love interests is laid before them at school, so it's easy to find potential mates. When you get older, you may feel out of practice, so it may be hard on your ego to admit you're attracted to someone. You may feel as if you're too dignified for dating. This is your ego getting in the way of love, and you need to shelve its voice. Instead, find a way of flirting, dating, and mating that is comfortable for you. As you begin to open your mind to dating, it won't be nearly as bad as you feared.
- *The older you get, the wiser you are.* As you age, you experience more of love's ups and downs and you acquire wisdom on the subject. You're inherently more discerning about who you'll spend time with, so you date more wisely and waste less time with someone unsuitable.
- *Older folks put up with less b.s.* Your standards get higher as you age, and your self-esteem goes up (according to University of California report by Richard W. Robins and K. H. Trzesniewski in 2005).[10] Therefore, you have more appropriate standards. Your b.s. meter is finely tuned, and you'll say no more easily to what won't work for you.

A MYTH ABOUT DATING WHEN YOU'RE OLDER

Myth: The older I get, the less attractive I'll be to the opposite sex.

Reality: I have not seen this to be true for either gender. I've seen countless older men date even older women. And young men often are captivated by older women while ignoring younger "babes." Many people prefer the maturity level of older people and have more in common with them as well. Love knows no age, and if you look around, you'll see how much truth there is in this.

When I hear this myth, it's usually reflective of someone's fears. If you've been telling yourself that you're over the hill and that no one will be interested in someone your age, this is your own belief that you need to work on. I have seen too many happy couples who connected later in life to believe that line of reasoning. Understand that you are wildly attractive to your One, no matter how many wrinkles you have or what your age is.

- *Aging singles are more independent and less likely to make someone else their source of happiness.* This concept was mentioned earlier and is worth noting again. The Universe doesn't support us in mistaking any other person as our source of happiness and satisfaction. No one can bear the kind of pressure it places upon them to label them the source of your happiness, the source of your support (even if you are financially relying upon them), or the source of anything important in your life. There is a greater Source (God, the Universe, a Higher Power), and if this person exits your life, you would continue on just fine without him or her. As an older single, you've spent years learning who you are and how to care for yourself. You've had to release a few people in your time. So the older you are, the less likely you are to make someone else your everything. This school of thinking is more prevalent with the young and makes dating much harder on them. Overall, the advantages to dating when you're older are far greater than the disadvantages.

AS YOU GET CLOSER

So you've found a person who you think is your One, and you're now dating. But it's not going at the pace you want it to. What do you do? The answer involves *trust*. Your pace of developing a relationship may not be the same as your partner's, and part of real love is honoring the other person's process. As long as the relationship remains dynamic, you can trust that it will continue to progress.

Are your insecurities coming up? Soothe them with the knowledge of just how powerful attachment is. If the two of you are getting closer and closer, rest assured that it will take more than you realize to drag you apart. There are two kinds of relationship insecurities. One has to do with unjustified fears. If she has given you no reason to feel insecure, then your problems lie within your own being, and you need to work on your jealousy issues. However, the second type of relationship insecurity is warranted. If your girlfriend is a big flirt and is engaged in surreptitious behavior that gives you cause to worry, you need to take a look at your relationship and evaluate whether she is right for you after all. Her behavior could signal other, deeper issues.

The large majority of jitters I encounter are of the first variety, the unjustified insecurities. While I know you may feel vulnerable as you open your heart, you can calm yourself and have faith that the Universe won't meet you only halfway, nor three-quarters of the way, but *all* the way. This is the truth. You really will have full-on love, not just something briefly waved under your nose only to be jerked away.

Love will lead the way, and I have seen many seeming problems between a couple simply dissolve. People who are continents away from each other somehow come together. If you stay focused on the love and the continued connection, trust that everything will work out.

In chapter 10, I talk about how to solidify and maintain a wonderful relationship. As you connect with your soulmate, make sure to go over the points in this final chapter. They will help as the two of you move into a deeper commitment. Above all, remember that if you two are soulmates, nothing can keep you apart. You will end up together, so rest assured and trust in love.

I affirm that dating is becoming an entirely new and delightful experience for you. Your attitude has changed, and so has the process of dating for you. Your union with your soulmate is delightful and without stress.

9

Countdown to Love Liftoff

The Ninth Magnet: Get Ready for the Ride of Your Life

There is a principle that I call "divine timing." It is what will put you and your soulmate at the right place at the right moment to come together. I have seen divine timing at work with almost every soulmate relationship that has blossomed under my guidance. What does this mean for you? It means you may have to wait awhile for your soulmate. Listed below are some of the reasons you might have to wait for your soulmate:

- Your soulmate isn't available for you yet—maybe he's in a relationship at the moment or hasn't yet moved to your city.

- One of you has some unfinished business.
- The Universe is still engineering your connection. For example, in two months you and he will be heading to the same vacation destination.
- The Universe knows that a delay can make you cherish love when it comes so that you'll never take it for granted.
- This is your time to deepen your faith in circumstances that haven't yet manifested and in the Divine.
- You are being given the chance now to work on your issues and your areas of growth so that this relationship with your soulmate can be drama-free.
- You may have blocks you still need to work through that are delaying your soulmate's arrival (you'll find more on this later in this chapter).
- Some other area of your life may need your attention right now. It could be a child you're raising or your career. The time is not yet ripe for your love.

Whatever the timing for you two may be, patience is valuable right now. While you are waiting, practice patience, because the time for meeting your soulmate may not be right just yet. But instead of being desperate, learn to enjoy the ride and be happy now, even before you're in the amazing relationship that's on its way. Patience is, of course, considered a virtue, and if you easily get impatient, this is your chance to change.

The book *A Course in Miracles*, states,

"The only thing that will bring **immediate** effect is infinite **patience**."

Why do you need patience? First, it will keep you from driving yourself crazy while you wait for your soulmate to appear. Second, it will stop you from taking the wrong actions out of desperation. As previously discussed, you want to avoid desperation at all costs—it's not good for you and does the opposite of magnetizing love to you. When you're impatient, you may settle for the wrong person, try to force a fit that doesn't exist between you and someone else, or sabotage yourself in other ways.

Instead of getting antsy, honor each moment and dive fully into the "now." Date as much as you're comfortable with (in the way I've talked about in the previous chapter, which should make it fun for you), enjoy every moment, relish your single life, and make some space in your life for love. People who have trouble being patient will most likely grow up a bit during the waiting stage. Kids have no tolerance for delayed gratification. They want what they want *when* they want it. If you never learned how to wait for a payoff, this is your chance. Not only are you taking an important developmental step, but you are also ensuring that you end up with your soulmate. Delayed gratification allows the right person to come in and avoids the state of despondence in which people try to make something fit that isn't right. You can increase your patience level by exploring new interests, such as taking a class or beginning a new hobby (more on this later).

GETTING RID OF YOUR BLOCKS TO LOVE

While nothing can keep your soulmate from you, his arrival into your life can be *delayed* by blocks you may have, either knowingly or unknowingly. Now is the time to deal with these blocks. Here is a rundown of the most common blocks to love that people have and how to rid yourself of them.

Self-Worth Issues

You can't believe you are deserving of love, or you don't think you're good enough for anyone you would actually be attracted to. We discussed earlier in the book ways to boost your self-esteem and heal the part of you that feels lacking. Keep working on this. It can be a gradual process.

Blocked Sexual Energy

You've been alone too long or hurt too much and have shut down the sexual centers in your body, located in your hip and groin area. This seems to most often occur in people who haven't dated in years or who grew up in an environment of repression where sex was labeled bad. Unblocking your sexual energy doesn't involve any drastic changes. You can simply work on finding your inner flirt, which opens your sexual channels; take belly dancing or hip-hop lessons, two dance styles that get your hips going and your energy flowing (or just go out dancing regularly); or have a fling with someone who will serve as your opener, as discussed earlier.

Emotional Shutdown

Some people react to being hurt deeply by emotionally shutting down. This can be something that happened to you as an adult, or worse, as a child. If you've never had a long-term relationship as an adult, you may be one of those children who, because of neglect, simply shut down emotionally and is now more comfortable maintaining distance from others. This is a serious issue, and help (in the form of therapy or a support group) may be needed for you to open up. You can begin this process by making a concerted effort to let others in. Start by confiding in a trusted friend. Talk with your friend about what you're going through and maintain regular contact. Also, do some emotional healing work as described earlier in this book. Finally, force yourself to seek people you are attracted to and talk to them, opening up communication with them. Even if it leads nowhere, it is important for you to open pathways within yourself that have been blocked.

A Life Too Full

It is easy to fill your life with situations and circumstances that don't leave you open to love. Some of these include working too much of the time; being involved with someone for comfort even though you know there's no future in the relationship; being so consumed with single parenting that you leave no time for your own fun; and giving so much to others that you leave no room to concentrate on your own life. In their extremes, such situations can be avoidance mechanisms, because you are afraid to open yourself to the vulnerability of love. If you find yourself with a life that leaves no room for love, take steps to simplify your life and force yourself to take time to concentrate on social activities.

Cynicism

I spoke about this in chapter 1—you really need to watch your attitude about love. In our culture it's easy (and even cool) to adopt the prevailing mind-set that love is rare and doesn't last. Keep working to improve your beliefs about love, and surround yourself with cheerleaders who help you keep your outlook for the future sunny.

Attachment to Someone Else

This is the biggest block of all and is dealt with extensively in chapter 5. The fact is that if you are carrying a torch for someone, even if you think you still have room for your soulmate, your energy on a very subtle level puts up a "do not disturb" sign to prospective mates. I have worked with many people who, when they finally release, suddenly find swarms of interested suitors where there once was a dating desert. Do your release work in earnest if this is your block.

GET YOUR DUCKS IN A ROW

Now, during the time lag between sending out your soul call and uniting with your soulmate, is the perfect time to get your affairs in order. Once you fall in love, you'll find little time for the practical. You'll be too busy being swept up by love. Get your act together now, before love materializes.

Here are some steps you can take now to be prepared for your soulmate. When you embark upon your delicious romance, it's more fun not to have to worry about too many practical things. And indeed, many people almost leave the world behind in the delirium of discovering each other.

1. Pay all of your bills, get them organized, and set up an automatic draft or bill pay system if possible. When your mail piles up for weeks because you've been staying at his house, at least you'll know that your bills are still getting paid and your credit rating is safe.
2. Clean up and declutter your home. You may not have done this for a while, so do it now, while you have some time. If she opens your closet door, your belongings won't fall out and hit her in the face.
3. Make a few gourmet meals and freeze them. That way you'll have some instant dinners for the two of you and can forgo grocery shopping when you'd rather be together.
4. Spend time with friends and family now. I've rarely seen a couple in the flush of first love who don't disappear into their own world for a while. This is natural as you two discover your own dynamic (therefore, be understanding of friends who do this, too—cut them some slack if they lay low for a while with their new love).
5. Get extra underwear and essentials in case you skip doing laundry for a while. Attractive undergarments are especially nice in preparation for your One. Matching, flattering lingerie for women is good, and most guys look incredibly hot in boxer briefs.
6. Stock up on candles, romantic music, some champagne or sparkling cider with flutes, a robe, bubble bath, and other effects to make your place more romance-friendly. You'll be using them before you know it.
7. Look in your life for chores and tasks that you do each week that take up your time. Try to get ahead with them.

You'll be happy you did later on, as it will free you up to spend more time with your One.

HAVE FAITH

Let's say I was a really good psychic who had repeatedly predicted events that actually happened in your life. One day I told you, "You will meet your soulmate in short time. It is a done deal, so start yelling out your car window, 'Thank you God for my husband!'" No doubt this would make you feel reassured that love was really coming. You might even cease to have any doubts that you really do have a soulmate and that he was on his way into your life.

Even this minute you can realize that same truth simply by having faith. Faith is the best psychic there is. It is a deep knowing that all is well even when appearances might tell a different story at the moment. Faith can make you see beyond the seeming dating desert that is now in your life. Faith can give you the rock-solid assurance that your soulmate is on his or her way into your life *now*.

Faith can carry the day, even against all odds. Cultivate your faith and it will become easier for you to remain strong through your single days. You can have a ball once you know without a shadow of doubt that love is on its way into your life. I don't believe that faith has to be blind. It can be cultivated as you see the results of your prayers, your affirmations, and your emerging self-confidence. The Divine leads us to a deeper faith, and if you're keeping track, you'll see so many good results that you can no longer doubt. One great faith builder is to *notice* all of the ways that you have been supported by the Universe and the ways that your prayers have been answered. Noticing is important.

Homework: **Start noticing the serendipity in your life. As you do, more magical occurrences will begin to happen, following the principle of *What you focus on grows bigger.* Jot down descriptions of these magical occurrences in your Soulmate Journal. This will help to build your faith. Later, I ask that you begin a gratitude list, and you can definitely include serendipitous events that you've begun noticing on this list.**

So now I'm going to be your psychic. And what I have to say to you is this: *Love is on its way into your life.* Get ready for it, because here it comes! Know this and conduct yourself accordingly. Shout out your car window (even if everyone thinks you're crazy), "Thank you God for my husband [or wife]!" Have this faith and life will look different to you. This time lag until your One arrives will be rich with new understanding and preparation.

LIVE IT UP WHILE YOU'RE SINGLE

One day you will look back fondly on your single days, particularly if you can cherish them now. Having faith that love is on its way will keep you from feeling desperate or depressed. It will give you a glow that can make your numbered single days quite fun.

Enjoy the fact that right now you get to sleep alone. For some singles sleeping by themselves can seem lonely, but when you spend years of your life sleeping next to someone who snores, or sleep in a bed that ends up crowded with kids by the end of the night, you may look fondly upon your glorious solo nights.

Take pleasure in being able to do what you want, when you want. It can be fun having no one to be accountable to. You are footloose and fancy-free. When you are no longer single, there is a certain amount of "checking in" that happens. This is endearing and a different kind of fun, but there are times when you may feel less free.

Enjoy the fact that you get to spend all of your discretionary money on yourself. Once you're married, your money may be earmarked for practical expenses, with little or nothing left for personal shopping whims. You may need to answer to your One about where the money goes. Your expenses as a couple will go up. When you have a family, your overhead increases even more. So savor each discretionary penny you spend.

Enjoy putting yourself first. When you are single, you get to think of yourself first. Many wedding vows include a promise to think of your spouse's welfare as at least as important as your own. If you have children, your first allegiance may be to them rather than your own well-being. For now, while you are single, bask in taking care of yourself as your sole responsibility.

All in all, there are advantages to being where you are right now. If you haven't fully reveled in your freedom, if you've been too busy trying to find your mate to appreciate your single life, now is the time to appreciate this stage and live it up.

KEEP YOUR THOUGHTS POSITIVE

If you would not characterize yourself as a happy person, now is the time to work on that. You can be happy right this minute, and you owe it to yourself to do so. A 2005 University of Michigan study found that people who experience a severe illness but are inherently happy revert to being just as happy as they were within three months of recovering.[11] By the same token, naturally unhappy people will return to being just as unhappy even after a major boost like winning the lottery. There is a growing body of evidence to suggest that in the long run our happiness levels are unaffected by either catastrophe or good fortune.

What does this mean for you? It means you need to learn to be happy *now*. It may not seem that easy to suddenly be happy, but it's not that difficult. I ask my clients to practice being grateful for what is in their lives. What you focus on expands, so if you turn your back firmly on anything that could make you upset, and focus on the good instead, then your life will change in a positive way. Are you short on reasons to be grateful? How about the fact that you are breathing right now and have the gift of sight to read this book? Start with that.

LEARN TO BE ALONE WELL

When I do a poll at my workshops, a majority of people raise their hands when I ask, "How many of you have trouble going places socially by yourself?" Sure, they'll go to the grocery or bookstore solo, but wouldn't dare be a party of one at a restaurant or show up at a social event unescorted.

If this sounds like you, now is the perfect time to overcome this limiting thought pattern. And it is limiting. You've probably skipped parties or meals just because you didn't have someone to go out with. What it takes is a reframing

YOU CAN BE HAPPY NOW

To break a habit of being unhappy, you need to learn to reprogram your thinking. Here are some suggestions on how to become happier now.

1. *Make it a habit to notice five good happenings or occurrences in your life every day.* Write them down in your Soulmate Journal every night before going to bed. They can be quite small. Examples:

   - There was no line in the post office today.
   - I had a really great lunch.
   - My most attractive coworker winked at me today at work.

   It may take awhile to become proficient at recognizing and recording the good things that happen in your daily life, but eventually you will become attuned to looking for the positive. And because what we focus on expands, you will begin to find yourself with a list of longer than five good things per day. This is a perfect way to turn into an optimist, seeing the glass as half full.
2. *When an occurrence is bringing you down or causing you worry, take a moment to examine why you are being affected in a negative way.* Write down the meaning that you are ascribing to this particular situation. Examples:

   Situation: The guy you went out with isn't calling right away for a second date.

Your Interpretation: You blew it somehow, and he's never going to call.
The Truth: He does call in a week. A big project came up at work, and he was so consumed he didn't have time to think about his social life until he got a handle on the job at hand. Or maybe he doesn't call, but you're able to remember that you do have a soulmate out there and clearly he's not it, so that's okay. You move on without turning one forgotten call into the thought that you'll never get love.

Situation: You get a speeding ticket.
Your Interpretation: You're going to owe massive amounts of money, your insurance will go up, and you may have to go to court. How could you have been so stupid?
The Truth: You pay the ticket, and it's not that much (it's only money). Your insurance doesn't go up, because it was only the first ticket on your record. Almost everyone gets a speeding ticket in their lifetime, and since they all can't be stupid, neither are you.

The fact is that almost everything you worry or get upset about will blow over and be forgotten in six months. Look back to six months ago and see if you can remember what you were upset about then. Mark Twain once said, "I have been through some terrible things in my life, some of which actually happened." No longer waste your time dealing with imagined consequences. Instead, limit yourself to dealing with the issue at hand without projecting a dire future. Waiting for the other shoe to drop is no way to enjoy life. It will take work to unravel patterns of worry or overreacting, but the effort is worth it.

3. *Take life less seriously.* Humor is not only a happiness trigger, but as Norman Cousin's research found, it actually boosts one's health.[12] If you are an overly serious sort of person, look for ways to spur your sense of humor. Watch funny shows on television, memorize jokes or ask people if they have a good one, and search for the humor in your life. Add to your list of five good things per day at least one occurrence that was funny.
4. *Meditate, do yoga, or undergo hypnosis.* Any of these three activities alter your brain waves, sending your brain into an alpha or relaxed state. According to the book *The Relaxation Response*, research shows that if you give your brain these "time outs," you circumvent your fight-or-flight response and actually lower your blood pressure.[13] You become a calmer, more content person by doing these activities

of your thought processes. People who won't go out alone think along these lines:

"Everyone will be thinking I have no friends."
"It'll be me and twenty couples at the restaurant. I'll be painfully dateless for the world to see."

"I won't have anyone to talk to, and it'll be really uncomfortable."

"It's bad enough I'm single, but I don't have to put that fact on display."

It's time for an attitude adjustment. No one is thinking these ideas if you don't. You're simply projecting your own fears or insecurities onto the nameless "they," whoever happens to be around and might judge you. In truth, only *you* are judging you. I know plenty of secure, well-liked people who go out alone simply because of the freedom factor. They don't want to be tied down to others. Instead of worrying that they will be thought of poorly, they don't care at all what anyone else thinks.

I've worked with several clients on healing an inability to go out alone, and the results have been life-changing. Chrissie's first assignment was to take herself out to a restaurant. She was encouraged to bring a good book to enjoy. Naturally, she found the experience excruciating. It seemed everyone else in the restaurant was on a date. She was painfully aware of her single status, but stuck it out and even enjoyed reading the book and being served at the same time. But every time she looked up, she felt like everyone was staring at her, labeling her a loser. We kept working together to overcome her self-consciousness. She went to party after party, event after event alone, and a wonderful transformation took place. She began to care less about what other people might think and learned to enjoy herself and the freedom of flying solo. As Chrissie later said:

THE LADY IN THE RESTAURANT

A striking woman came into a restaurant alone. Dressed well, she held herself in such a way that it was hard not to notice her. She was self-assured, comfortable in her own skin, charming. She asked for a table for one. When seated, she ordered, pulled out some work to do, and went about her business.

You could see that people were enchanted by her. The waiter often lingered at her table, engaging her in conversation. She laughed, smiled, and conversed with him and with others who came by the table, including a manager, a busboy, the hostess, and even other waiters not assigned

"I realized I adored being alone when I was dancing by myself, in a flowing dress, at an outdoor concert. I had seen several friends there, and at that moment a song I loved came on, and I found myself moving to it. I must have had five men approach me afterward wanting to ask me out. One said I was a vision from heaven dancing there alone in the crowd. I felt set free, that I needed no one to validate who I was. I've never forgotten that moment."

Chrissie is no longer single. She is married with children and rarely gets alone time. But every now and then, she needs to get out and float around on her own, unfettered. She now has the assurance to do that and revel in it. It is quite attractive to behold.

to her table. Other diners wondered who she was, and a man at another table sent over an aperitif. She held up her glass, toasted him with a mouthed thank-you, and went back to her work. When she left, the room suddenly felt less dynamic.

This is a true story. I was in college at the time and was working as a waiter at this restaurant. I wondered at my own inability to go out alone and how this woman did so with such ease and grace. I struggled to get to a point in my life where I could have such self-confidence. I now can go out alone and feel comfortable.

BEGIN TO CREATE YOUR WORLD NOW

Imagine the world that you and your soulmate will inhabit, and start creating it now even before he or she appears on the scene. Firm up your friendships with people who are supportive. Begin communicating at the deepest level possible with those who are close to you right now. In the next chapter, in which I talk about your relationship once you are with your One, I detail the eight levels of communication. As you read that section of the chapter, think about how you could start relating more deeply with others now. Allow your intuition to blossom.

In *The New Single Woman*, author E. Kay Trimberger pooh-poohs the notion of soulmates being needed to fulfill one's life, and I agree. Although she and I have different points, I believe you shouldn't put life on hold but should instead live fully while waiting for love to present itself to you. You will be much more interesting, and you will have less growth to achieve with your mate if you are already quite independent. The best relationships are those in which each party has some independence, a life outside of their marriage. You'll find more about this in the next chapter. The point is that you need to learn to be happy now.

Having said this, I think Eckhard Tolle makes an important observation about love in his book *The Power of Now*. He notes that even the most spiritually evolved person may still have a longing in his heart for love. It is foolish to think that if you are simply enlightened enough, you will no longer wish for a mate. Other than the occasional person who was meant to be alone in this lifetime, most of us have internal space that will not be satisfied until we meet our soulmate. This is what propels us forward into his arms. So while you learn to be happy alone, don't judge yourself if there is still a corner of your heart that remains discontent. This is the empty love cup that can be filled only by your soulmate, and it is a good thing.

❤ MAGNETIZATION STEP 9 ❤
PREPARE FOR THE RIDE OF YOUR LIFE

After you read this chapter, make the following four lists in your Soulmate Journal, giving at least a page to each one. Feel free to refer back to this chapter to aid in creating these lists.

- Things I Need to Do to Get Ready for Love
- Fun Things I Should Be Doing Now while I'm Still Single
- Three Things I Can Do to Be Happier Right Now
- Ways I Can Begin to Create My World Now

Also journal at least one page concerning the level of patience you have in waiting for love.

Get out your calendar and block out time to carry out at least two items from each of the four lists in the coming week. Go back to these lists to add to them or to note your progress in following through on these lists of actions as you take steps to fulfill them.

YOU DID IT!

This is the end of the nine Magnetization Steps, and you have successfully completed your magnetization process. You should feel different, having gone through this program, and I affirm that you are a powerful attractant for your One.

Continue to keep yourself in a good place, referring back to various chapters as needed. For example, once you schedule a date to go out with someone, reread Magnetization Step 8 before the date to refresh yourself on your new way of dating, and look at your Soulmate Journal notes for this topic as well. Or if you're having a bad moment, refer back to Magnetization Step 6 for how to shore yourself back up. If you get hooked on the wrong person, go back to Magnetization Step 5 to release and move on. You can continue to add to your journal, including the lists you've started on various love topics. Continued journaling will enhance your expansion into love.

To get a better template in your head of just how wonderful your soulmate relationship will be, keep reading. The final chapter of this book describes this match from heaven and offers ways of making it even better, dealing with any issues that come up as you embark upon this wonderful adventure into love.

I affirm that something real has happened as you have participated in this program. In the coming days and weeks, you will see the evidence of all the good work you've done. Love is on its way, and the time of your life is directly ahead for you.

10

Once It's Happened

A Relationship from Heaven

Two of the often-repeated concepts about relationships that I dislike the most are:

Relationships are hard work.
You have to really work at it to make a marriage last.

No, no, no! I'd like to take the word "work" out of association with relationship. After a breathtaking courtship, an exhilarating ride into each other's arms, is that the best we can hope for? I don't think so. As I mentioned earlier, what we believe acts as true until we substitute that belief with a better one. So can we please chuck out the notion of relationships as hard work once and for all? Instead, believe we can have exactly what the title of this chapter describes, *A Relationship from Heaven.* Wouldn't you rather have that? What does a Relationship from Heaven look like? Since it's a relationship with your soulmate, it's more harmonious than any other love relationship you've ever known. Here are some characteristics of the Relationship from Heaven:

- You have a free-flowing, smooth relationship without stress or discord.
- You have a lot of fun together.
- You are each other's favorite company, best friends, and confidantes.
- You reach a level of communication at which words are often unnecessary.
- You connect deeply and can talk about anything.
- You strengthen each other and support each other.
- You have enormous physical chemistry even after years of being together.
- Your relationship remains dynamic and interesting.
- You share a spiritual practice together or discuss deep issues with each other.
- You help to heal each other of any lingering wounds and encourage growth.

If this sounds good to you, then affirm it is what you will have. Keep the Relationship from Heaven as a template in your mind for your own relationship. Yes, all relationships do require a certain amount of input and presence, but with your soulmate this becomes easy and is *not work*.

AVOIDING THE LETDOWN

The journey we make to come together is terribly exciting. The initial electricity of connecting and the mating dance that follows are intrinsically breathtaking. Here are some of the stages we go through as we begin our soulmate journey together:

- Learning that the other person is safe emotionally
- Becoming comfortable with each other's emotional patterns
- Finding the right fit as a couple, learning each other's dynamics and our own together
- Enjoying mind-blowing sex
- Becoming closer and closer as the love grows

Compared to what has come before, actual couplehood can be a letdown. It can even get boring. But only if you let it. Some relationship experts claim that a courting relationship is different from a marriage, and while there are some obvious differences (like you've committed to being together now, so any question of faithfulness is eradicated), the courtship doesn't need to end. Many people falter once the initial excitement of finding their One begins to fade. There is a physiological, biochemical reaction that goes along with falling in love. This high can diminish as you settle into each other. It's probably a good thing to let the relationship slow down, because your system will need a break, time to

UNKNOWINGLY SOULMATES

Quint was married to Sally for twenty-three years before he realized she was his soulmate. He always knew they were meant to be together and couldn't imagine them being apart. But he wouldn't have said she was his soulmate. In fact, he feared that maybe he had missed his true love. Quint and Sally had three children together and went through the ups and downs of relationship, always working out problems and trying to improve their communication.

One day after their children were grown and out of the house, the two were sitting at dinner when Quint looked into Sally's eyes and had the oddest sensation. "My whole body warmed up as we gazed at each other, and I remembered how much we had shared together. I recognized that Sally had been my soulmate all along, and that maybe I was just too scared to acknowledge that fact." This realization took their relationship to a whole new level, and it continues to get better each day. Quint has never been happier.

integrate your new life together. However, in a soulmate relationship, what I find to be amazing is that time and time again, the chemical rush returns, fueled by an ever-changing, evolving relationship together. This is what an endless honeymoon looks like.

One way to avoid the letdown is to keep moving forward. While routine can bring security, it can also bring boredom. To avoid any ruts, keep moving toward your visions together as a couple. There is a saying that I love by the Reverend Michael Beckwith (the founder and minister of my spiritual community, Agape): "We are pushed by our pain until we are pulled by our vision." Rather than forget your vision together and become pushed by the pain of growing apart or getting bored, keep your eye on what your next step as a couple is. Embrace growth, adventure, and change, for they keep things fresh and the two of you moving forward . . . together.

Each stage of a relationship has its own arc. As long as you are growing together, the relationship will remain dynamic and exciting. It can become something even more now that you've found each other and have agreed that you will walk your path together. Here are some tips for staying in ecstasy with your soulmate for a lifetime:

1. ***Vow that as a couple, you will not stagnate.*** Agree on this. Set the intention that together, you will remain dynamic, growing (both individually and together) and fully engaged in life with one another.
2. ***Hold on loosely.*** Allow a certain amount of freedom in the relationship. Understand between the two of you that it's okay to follow your own interests and not be joined at the hip. Everyone has their own level of closeness, from the Italian woman who grew up in a family of twelve and has a difficult time being alone to the reclusive man who finds it a big adjustment to be with his soulmate. Find what works for you, but don't allow yourselves to be clingy, overly jealous, or constraining with each other. The best relationships flourish in an

environment of freedom, where every day you're together because you *choose* to be together.

3. ***Let go of past insecurities.*** I have seen in my work that the emotional bond between two people in a romantic couple is much stronger than most people really realize. Breaking a relationship apart is not easy. And breaking a soulmate relationship apart is impossible. If you have been cheated on or abandoned in the past, it is time to let that hurt go. It's not fair to bring it into this relationship, and any fears that something similar could happen again are unwarranted. Letting go of this worry will free you to explore, to grow freely without a shadow hanging over your union. For past hurts, do the release and forgiveness work described in chapter 5, and use the techniques for healing your insecurity that are outlined in chapter 4.
4. ***Be supportive of each other.*** A soulmate relationship is one in which you build each other up, not tear each other down. Your mutual love strengthens you both. It is a sanctuary in which you get nurtured and then go out into the world fortified to fulfill your purpose.
5. ***Establish a zero tolerance policy for badmouthing.*** Ask your friends to never say a bad word about your mate to you or to anyone. I actually include this instruction to the guests at the wedding ceremonies that I perform. Words are so powerful that someone verbally tearing down your partner can have a real undermining effect, no matter how much you love her. In a sacred relationship, ask friends and family to support your relationship always. If you find someone weakening it on purpose or

unknowingly, set him straight. Cut him off the minute you realize he is speaking ill of your partner, and remind him that you don't want to hear anything bad about her. And make sure you don't speak ill about your spouse to anyone, either. Beyond processing your feelings with a best friend who highly respects your relationship or with a therapist, be careful about how you present your spouse to others. Tearing him down when you've had a falling out can seriously undermine your relationship.

6. ***Create time alone together for dates, sexual liaisons, and simply enjoying each other's company.*** This is especially important for parents of young children, because it's easy to let time alone fall by the wayside. Have sex in a variety of places to keep the spice in your love life, and always try new things. Sometimes, avoiding intimacy is a way of protecting yourself. It is important to realize that you no longer need to avoid intimacy. You are in a safe relationship now, and you can let your guard down and be close.
7. ***Never, ever take this gift from God for granted.*** If you have been alone for years, waiting for your love, it is easier to stay appreciative of this miracle that has come into your life. Other people may need to make a conscious effort to maintain their gratitude. Make sure you express your awe of your soulmate regularly with kind words, compliments, flirting, and physically with hugs, kisses, and back rubs. None of us knows how long we get to be together (death has its own unpredictable timing), so it is critical to cherish every moment we have with our One.

8. ***Keep growing, keep evolving together.*** Every now and then a married person comes to me in horror, saying, "She's not the same person I married. She's changed," as though it were a mortal sin. It is not reasonable to expect your soulmate to remain the same. The only constant in life is change, and this is true of each human being as well. We want to continue to grow, to learn, to become wiser. Be supportive of your partner's changes, and keep informed of them. Ask your mate to support your own growth as well, and share regularly what is going on with you—what's happening at work, among your friends, as well as your thoughts, hopes, and dreams. This will enrich both of your lives and keep the two of you connected as you continue on your journey together.
9. ***Retain your awe of your soulmate.*** There is a temptation to learn someone's habits, get to know them up to a certain level, and then let yourself become bored. This is a false construction perpetrated by a shallow society. It is not possible to get bored with another human being. Why? Because there is no reaching the bottom of another being, even if you've lived together for fifty years. Don't overlook the fact that your mate is an endless mystery, one that you can spend decades exploring and never get tired of.
10. ***Don't make this person your source on any level.*** No person on this planet can ever be your source, and to expect this from another person is unrealistic and unbalanced. So if you are depending on your soulmate for your happiness, for money and anything else, you

need to give up that notion. If you are being supported by your spouse, that is okay. What I'm talking about is more of an energetic neediness than your financial setup. Get in the habit of letting go of such thinking if it arises. No one can be everything to you—not even your soulmate. It puts a lot of pressure on another being to be someone else's whole world, and this pressure is not healthy for the relationship. So if he can't always be there for you, simply say to yourself, "He is not my source," release the tendency to pity yourself, and the right support will show up, even when it can't be your mate.

11. ***Let your relationship be natural and spontaneous.*** Control in our lives is mostly an illusion and never more so than when it comes to relationships. There is no way for you to predict just how your relationship will grow, and so projecting into the future is a waste of time. Don't try to put your relationship in a neat, little box or become disappointed if it doesn't go just the way you'd hoped. If you let go of control, all sorts of wonderful twists and turns will happen that can keep it fresh and exciting. This is the opposite of "working" at a relationship, and therefore, it's much more fun.

12. ***Understand that no one will love you exactly as you want them to.*** It is important to accept that your spouse will love you in his own way. It may not be just the way you want it, but the more you recognize his own brand of expressing his feelings, the more you can let go of having your way. It doesn't matter if he can't express himself just the way you would like, as long as he shows

you he loves you. Brenda lived with Matt, and she was quite happy except for one thing: Matt could never say, "I love you," which was a source of pain for her. One day when they were making love, Brenda had a breakthrough. She wanted so badly to hear those words, but realized that she could say them to herself. And she silently did. She also thought back to earlier that night

AN EXCELLENT HONEYMOON ACTIVITY

Many companies have a mission statement that sets the tone for their business. And many people set forth their intentions on their birthday or at the beginning of each year. Your honeymoon is meant to be a time when you two recover from the wedding and come together for the first time as a married couple. Rituals are powerful, and going through a marriage or commitment ceremony is a rite of passage that makes you feel different. You get to practice hearing the phrase "my wife" or "my husband" trip easily off of your tongue. It's great fun!

The honeymoon is an ideal time to decide what the tone of your marriage will be and set some intentions. Take some quiet moments to work together on a Marriage Purpose Statement, and either incorporate some intentions into the statement or write them separately. Feel free to use any of the points in this chapter in this statement. Here is an example: *We intend to have an endless honeymoon, to establish a peaceful, loving home as our sanctuary, and to* when Matt had spent more than two hours rubbing her, something he often did. Brenda understood that this was one of many ways that Matt told her he loved her, but she had been missing it. He would never be verbally demonstrative, but he did demonstrate his love every day in other ways. This healed the issue for Brenda.

The more you can look for and understand the ways

get as close as two people ever were. The purpose of our union is to love each other and to lift up the planet with our love. Our relationship is trouble-free and shepherds us into a state of being in which love is everywhere we look.

Include your names in the statement as well as the date, and both of you should sign it. There is great power in formalizing your intentions by writing them down in a Marriage Purpose Statement. No detail is too small or petty to include in this statement. You never have to share it with anyone else—it is for the two of you. You can include plans for a family and how that will look, plans for a home, and anything else you see as part of your vision for your lives together and your purpose for being together.

This process will enrich your honeymoon and provide a greater bond between the two of you. Even if you don't marry, for whatever reason, but still make a long-term commitment, some sort of trip or retreat to celebrate your commitment is a good idea. And again, this process can help to strengthen you two as a couple. The results are quite magical!

your love demonstrates his or her caring for you, and the less you are set on having it your way, the happier you will be in the relationship.

THE UNCONVENTIONAL RELATIONSHIP

Every relationship has its own dynamics, and the two of you must see what yours are, without regard to anyone else's. Your union will not be like any one you had before, nor will it be like your parents' or your best friend's. For some couples, the relationship can be unconventional and yet work beautifully.

When Linda and Harry were dating, they realized they had come to a major impasse. Linda was passionately attached to her cats, but Harry was highly allergic to cat dander. They didn't let this seeming nonnegotiable item get in their way. Harry bought the condo next to his and moved Linda in after they married. She got to keep her cats, and they got to be together anyway. They adore their unconventional setup. They love having their own spaces as well as having each other near enough that they get to sleep together every night.

If your relationship looks like no one else's, that's okay. It will be set up to support the two of you as a couple for the highest good. If other people criticize, it's an opportunity for you to release caring what anyone else thinks and to tell them that they need to support your union, not tear it down. Let your marriage develop as it will, and if it's not "normal," who cares? It will be right for the two of you.

A HIGHER PURPOSE

A popular notion these days is that a relationship enters your life in order to teach you and help you grow. This idea is definitely a step in the right direction as opposed to the old-fashioned notion of riding off into the sunset and living happily ever after, never having to deal with a single issue that might arise. But while it's true that relationships can accelerate the growth of each individual, this is not a relationship's highest purpose. I urge you to grow together, to be willing to help heal each other's wounds and work on getting rid of any bad behaviors that interfere with your closeness.

But as I mentioned, there is an even loftier purpose for soulmate love, including your own. As you open to your soulmate, you are traveling toward a union that is not only the most effortless you've ever had, but is also one that is meant to inspire others and uplift the world around you. I believe the ultimate purpose of a soulmate relationship is to help others heal, to better the planet, and to shine the light of your love as a beacon to all.

Brook dated a string of men who didn't treat her well. A giving woman who taught seminars, she tended to attract men who wanted nurturing but gave her very little in return. Over and over again she got hurt. The drama of her dating life often took away from the energy she had for her seminars.

Finally, along came Lee, who, to her, was more handsome than any man she had dated, and who was as loving and nurturing as Brook. They discovered that they both had been looking for their soulmates, and would look at the stars at night, thinking that somewhere out there their One was looking at the same stars. Within a matter of months, Lee moved in with Brook, the couple became engaged, and then married. Lee was fully supportive of Brook's work and often helped her with it. She described him as her "rock," someone who steadied her through life's peaks and valleys. Brook's seminars took off, and it is clear that these two soulmates lift the world, not only through their work but also by providing a shining example of what real love looks like. Compared to the relationships they had in the past, the two are in awe of how easy this union is.

How good can it get for you? Won't it be fun to find out? I believe that the sky is the limit and that you can expect more than you could ever dream of.

FROM CRAZY LOVE TO HARMONY

In chapter 5 I talked about *crazy love* relationships. It is rare, but every now and then a crazy love relationship is a soulmate union. If you marry someone with whom you have crazy love, a highly dramatic relationship, there are ways you can take the relationship from crazy love to a harmonious, mature relationship. By definition, your coming together will have been intense.

Transforming your bond to something more solid begins with a single step. You both must agree that this is what you want and be willing to take the steps to make it happen. Here are some other steps you both must agree to work on:

- *Quit doing damage.* Crazy love partners tend to do damage to each other. Because of their insecurity, they play games to try to make the other person jealous. They attack the other to cover up their own wounds. They threaten divorce or breaking up on a regular basis in order to get their own way. You need to adopt a zero tolerance policy with regard to such behavior and call each other to task if it happens. It is simply not possible for a relationship to flourish in such a volatile environment. And the make-up sex that often accompanies this destructive behavior, no matter how good, is simply not worth the emotional wringer you put each other through. You will have even better sex as you heal. You and your partner need to understand that you are edging closer to disaster each time you behave this way, and agree that because you want to stay together, you will learn a new way of relating that is more mature.

- *Learn to communicate honestly in a safe, vulnerable environment.* Communication is key. A low level of communication is game playing—jockeying for control by threats, withdrawing, or attacking. If you can put this defensive volleying aside, you can get to the root of what is really going on and change it. Rather than flirting your way through a cocktail party to make your husband jealous, you can instead tell him that his being away at work so much is making you insecure and that you're worried he doesn't care. If you've both agreed to change, he won't get defensive or take advantage of your honesty. Instead, he will be moved by the admission and reassure you that he still cares. See the box below for a description of the levels of communication and how to get to the upper levels in your relationship.

- *Surrender your agenda.* You must learn to love each other unconditionally—this is the highest level of love. And the only way to achieve unconditional love is to remove your partner from being a part of your identity. No longer see her as your wife, part of the perfect picture of your family. No longer see her as someone who will meet some of your needs and offer comfort. No longer do you need to change her into your idea of a perfect wife. Instead, see her as a human being with her own journey. Realize that you are extremely lucky to share part of this journey with her.

It is easy to find yourself having an agenda for your partner and how she fits into your life. Every communication can be tinged with your need to get something from her. But this doesn't work and makes her into little more than an object. It is necessary to honor her by surrendering your agenda and ask that she do the same for you. Assume that your needs will be met, but not necessarily by her. Be willing to trust that the Universe will support you so that you can remove such an awesome burden from her. This takes much of the pressure off of your relationship and allows a new, healthier dynamic to emerge. The strength of your union will multiply many times over through your willingness to take such a step.

- *Quit laying blame.* To make yourself the victim by pinning your current problems on forces outside of your control is to behave at one of the lowest levels of being there is. Rarely is any situation simple enough to trace a definite cause for it. I have noticed a tendency in insecure people to blame themselves, taking on far more responsibility than is theirs, which is an egotistical thing to do, believe it or not.

  Also common in crazy love couples is blaming each other regularly for circumstances in their lives. As I said, it's rare that someone is totally to blame for a situation, and, blaming is a way of making yourself a victim and dodging your own responsibility for what has happened. Catch your knee-jerk reactions of blaming your mate, and instead take a breath. Think about other ways of working out your problems. It is more productive to express your hurt or disappointment over a situation rather than allow anger to overcome your emotions. You can ask your partner for cooperation in the future, but at the same time, make sure you own up to your part in creating it.
- *Learn to avoid taking someone else's words or actions personally.* No matter how personal it may feel to you when your spouse hurts you, the truth is that the pain she is expressing is not about you. It is her own pain that is coming out. Until we heal ourselves, our pain is from long-past hurts, most from our childhood days. Because you and your One are so close, being together may trigger these old

LEVELS OF COMMUNICATION

1. *Violence:* When you're physically abusing someone, pushing, shoving, slapping, or hitting, you're definitely communicating. You're just not sending a very good message and you're not sending it in a good way. Obviously, such behavior is to be avoided. Violence, even one time, is reason to get out of the relationship.
2. *Verbal/Emotional Abuse:* Any time someone insults another, puts her down, or calls her a name, this is verbal abuse. Examples of emotional abuse are denigrating someone to another within earshot of him, giving someone the cold shoulder, or yelling. None of these ways of communicating are acceptable in a good relationship.
3. *Posing/Posturing/Game Playing:* Trying to make someone jealous, pretending to be disinterested, putting on airs, or making a spectacle of yourself to get someone's attention fall into this realm. Many of us are guilty of engaging in such behavior at times, but you should be mature enough in your relationship not to have to resort to such indirect, hurtful ways of getting a point across.
4. *Arguing:* Believe it or not, this is a step up from the first three levels of communication I've described. Why? Because at least you are in direct conversation with each other instead of making a power play with immature behavior. I believe it is good to get over any fear you have about conflict and realize that arguing can sometimes be very helpful. If you avoid arguments, you limit communication. Worse, it's easy for someone to take advantage of you

by using arguments to make you back down if you shy away from confrontation.

At its lowest level arguing is merely two people hurling accusations at each other, yelling without hearing the other. There is no point to this type of arguing, and if you find yourself in this situation, it's best to stop talking at once until the other person does, too. Very little true communication can take place in such an unconscious argument. However, there *is* a way of arguing that can be productive and bring you two closer together. By using the Fair Fight Rules outlined later in this chapter, you can achieve such a result, where you both feel heard and you work things out for a greater understanding of each other.

5. *Discussing:* This level of communication is where crazy love ends and harmony begins. When the two of you are able to communicate with rational discussions, an equal give and take of thoughts and opinions, and effective listening, your relationship can greatly improve.
6. *Understanding/Acceptance:* A breakthrough in communication occurs when you find yourself understanding each other better. This is achieved through nonjudgmental listening and heartfelt expression. To get to this level of communication, you must put aside your own agenda and try to comprehend where your mate is coming from, what he is going through, and what he wants. You both must be willing to surrender your own agenda to reach understanding. Sometimes all it takes to heal a rift is a bit of understanding.

7. *Loving:* Loving communication is palpable. You can almost reach out and touch it. It is in the eyes, in the voice, in body language. It is an energy that changes the air around two people. We all recognize it when we see it, and you and your partner can have it, too, by vowing to approach each other in a space of love as much as you can. Your tone of voice, a slight touch, or a wink are enough to communicate your love. If you can agree to always express yourself from your heart first before addressing any concern, you will achieve this level of communication.

   Example: Before they put their crazy love behind them, when Landon returned from work, Miriam would greet him with a list of everything that went wrong during the day and basically dump the kids on him so that she could have a moment of peace. She had to learn instead to show him how

wounds. Even when she is lashing out at you, you can learn not to react, but instead offer compassion for the emotional bruises she is revealing to you. This isn't easy, but it is more constructive than taking her outburst personally. How can you do this? Here are some suggestions:

- Try not to immediately lash back when your partner does or says something that hurts you. Instead, take a moment to breathe and recover from the initial feelings you may be having.

happy she was to see him (which she was). She practiced greeting him with a hug and a kiss and asking him how his day was before sharing any of her own woes. This made all the difference to their relationship, and now it is much smoother.

8. *Communion:* The more closeness you can allow, the more you two will begin to intuit what the other is thinking, having the same thought at the same time (My husband and I are no longer surprised when this happens with us. We call this a "marriage moment"). This level of communication can keep expanding until you communicate nonverbally with many of those people who are closest to you. If your family expands beyond the two of you, a force can take over the family that is a powerful unifier, a sense of Oneness and deep connection. This is delicious. It is powerful when you often find yourselves knowing what the other person is thinking or feeling.

- As you take a step back, try to understand where your mate is coming from. Remind yourself that her upset isn't about you, but instead reveals some of her own pain.
- Allow your love to calm down before discussing the issue further. At this point, ask questions to better understand what is going on, draw a gentle boundary if you feel her treatment of you is unacceptable, and calmly discuss the issue.

To continue learning not to take things personally, I recommend reading the book *The Four Agreements,* by Don Miguel Ruiz. One of the four agreements is not taking things personally, and he discusses this concept in great depth.

- *Work on your own baggage.* The final step in healing your crazy love is to own your problems and issues and work on healing them. You two wouldn't have crazy love if both of you didn't have some wounds to recuperate from. It can be tempting to assume that you're the saint and he's the sinner, but if you didn't have problems as well, you wouldn't be involved in a crazy love relationship. Get into therapy or a support group. Pray, meditate, attend church, and read uplifting or self-help literature. Both of you should agree that you will do your part by ditching the baggage that gets in the way of a harmonious relationship.

As you take these steps to heal your crazy love, miracles will abound, and you can enter a much more fulfilling relationship than you two had together before now.

Your goal is to stay in the higher realms of communication as much as possible. We all have our bad days and can revert to lower levels, but the more you practice, the more you can avoid falling into those levels. The lower levels of communication are not productive and won't give you what you want, which is a loving, stable relationship.

ALLOWING EACH OTHER'S PROCESS

When I was going through my practitioner training, I learned a maxim that made seeing clients much easier, and it also can make relationships flow more smoothly.

Don't take away another person's process.

What does this mean? It alludes to the fact that we all have our way of learning, and we must be left to it. Anyone who has children understands that no matter how much you preach to them, they're often going to learn the hard way. Learning through life experience is how each of us acquires the deepest wisdom. And everyone has his or her own different way of dealing with challenges and processing them.

When your partner has a problem, you can't fix it for him. This would be taking away his process. You can be supportive, take some of the load off of him in terms of household or family responsibilities, and listen compassionately when he needs to vent. But what you can't and mustn't do is interfere with his path to resolving the situation, whatever it may be.

Too often I see a spouse trying to interfere in something his mate is going through, and this serves no one. It stresses out the meddling partner and can come across as patronizing to the distressed spouse, as though she can't solve it by herself. Your best course of action is to stay out of your partner's situation unless your advice is sought. This can be freeing for you both and helps to create a better relationship.

When your partner is going through a challenge or upset, you can also choose not to take it on. This means that no matter how much suffering your partner is going through, you won't let it get you down. It's not that you don't have compassion, it's just that you need to take care of yourself. It doesn't serve either one of you to get involved in something that is not yours to deal with. You are more useful to the relationship if you can remain centered and neutral. My client Marsha is a good example. She had been married to Fred for ten years when he got laid off and began searching for another job. Marsha arranged for Fred to work with a business coach and she even enrolled him in a career class to try and help. She got overly involved in his day-to-day search for a position. Busy herself with her own job and kids, she found herself so stressed out that she came to me for help. I pointed out to her that her best efforts with Fred had not borne any fruit and that she was taking on more than was comfortable for her. Gradually, Marsha was able to let go of Fred's situation and allow him to work it out for himself, which he did. She realized that she was trying to "fix" his situation rather than trust that he could find his way on his own. This was a freeing step for her, and after that, she was able to let Fred's process be his own.

ALMOST EVERYONE HATES THEIR SPOUSE ON CERTAIN DAYS

I was startled when I first noticed a phenomenon among the happily married couples I interviewed. They all mentioned that they had felt hatred for each other during certain times. As I work with more and more pairs, this trend worries me less. Unless you are the most evolved person on the planet, you are still growing and releasing your "baggage." Being close with another person is a sure-fire method of bringing up any unhealed issues within you. So it is natural that your beloved would be the one to push your buttons from time to time.

In my work I've seen that the best way to resolve such strong feelings is to own them as your own. It is never about the partner. You are just projecting your own unhappiness onto your spouse. Explore these emotions to discover their real roots, which are not related to your spouse. Talk to your mate about what you are experiencing, and be honest. This provides a tremendous release of the bad feelings. As you work through the feelings that underlie the hatred, your ill will toward your spouse will dissipate, and you will find yourself in love again.

"Love will have the final word."

—from "Trust Love"
by Rickie Byars Beckwith
and Rev. Michael Beckwith

I love these words. They turn the idea of one-upmanship and winning an argument on its ear. They suggest that he who loves the most wins. If you can remember that, it will change the way you relate, the way you feel about arguing, and the dynamic of your marriage. Rather than trying to

FAIR FIGHT RULES

Many therapists have a set of Fair Fight Rules that they give their clients. I mentioned them in the "Levels of Communication" box. Here is my version. Remember, learning not to fight is the best policy. However, when or if a disagreement arises, use these guidelines to get through the situation easily and damage-free. Go so far as to get out this book and go over these rules before you talk. You will learn a new and valuable way to resolve differences.

1. *Wait until you cool down to engage in a discussion with your partner.* The worst time to deal with a disagreement is in the heat of anger.
2. *Begin by telling him or her that you need to talk.* Together, pick a time and place that are neutral.
3. *Start the discussion by telling your mate that you're upset but want to work out the problem.* Remind him or her of your love.
4. *Don't use accusatory language.* Don't say "you did this" and "you made me feel that." Put everything in terms of "I." "I felt like you . . . ," "I was upset when you . . . ," "I think you . . ."
5. *Don't use inflammatory language.* Don't curse or call each other names.
6. *Confine your fight to the issue at hand.* Don't drag in the past or every mistake the other person ever made.
7. *Don't raise your voice.* Yell beforehand on your own (maybe into a pillow?), but screaming will produce nothing good when you two are arguing.

8. *Don't jump to conclusions.* Many times you will find that your anger is the result of a misunderstanding. Make sure you know just what happened and seek to understand it before getting upset.
9. *Don't assume that you know how your partner feels.* Ask him how he's feeling.
10. *Don't assume that everyone acts just like you would under the circumstances.* You have no idea how another human being processes information and situations and decides what to do. Everyone is different, and the way we behave is often not logical.
11. *Let your mate love you in his own, unique way, and take care to recognize his expressions of love, even when they're subtle.* He may not express his love for you the way you want, but you can't assume that he knows how you want him to love you.
12. *Practice forgiveness, and give a little more than you think you should* (short of letting yourself be emotionally or physically abused).
13. *Never make anyone else responsible for your happiness.* Don't make anyone else your source. It doesn't work. Therefore, your expectations for what your mate can do for you should be reasonable.
14. *Apologize easily, and take responsibility for your part of what went wrong.* Don't blame.
15. *Don't take things personally.* People do the best they can, and most words and behaviors that could be interpreted as hurtful are simply "blind spots" or issues arising within

the person that have nothing to do with you. See the tips earlier in this chapter on how to avoid taking things personally.

16. *Before you end the argument, decide how you can work together better next time.*
17. *End your fight in a space of love and forgiveness. Hug and kiss.* Fights not only allow you to work things out, but they also deepen your relationship and lead to a greater understanding of each other.
18. *To help prevent future fights, engage in regular spiritual practice either with or without your* One. Pray for her and for the relationship. Pray with her if you can. Set intentions together for your relationship. Meditate together.

win an argument, be the most loving, the quickest to forgive. Being the bigger person is the highest way. Knowing this comes in handy as you travel through life in love. Leading with love, finding love even in the most difficult situation is one of the keys to transforming your life from strife into one full of understanding, respect, and love.

As I work in the field of love, I see more and more soulmates who have been together for years. Before I believed in soulmates, all I saw were dysfunctional, unhappy marriages. This is a demonstration of the idea that what you believe acts as true until you substitute it with a higher belief. You find what you're looking for. When I was convinced that perfect love didn't exist, I saw dysfunction everywhere; but as soon

A SEVENTY-YEAR MARRIAGE

I recently met a man named Dudley at a party. Dudley is ninety-two years old. He told me that he had been married for close to seventy years and that his wife, Marian, died two years ago. As Dudley spoke of Marian and how much he missed her, it became clear to me that they were soulmates. He said that she was his best friend and that he is still learning to live without her. Shortly after Marian passed away, Dudley almost died, too. But he recovered and chose to keep on living. However, he seems to be immune to the countless female residents of his nursing home, who, I gather, tend to throw themselves at this fine man. Seventy years together, and still they never got enough of each other! This is what soulmate love looks like. A perfect footnote is that the party where I met Dudley was for his granddaughter, Christy, to celebrate her marriage to her own soulmate, Andrew. Clearly, Dudley's wonderful example influenced Christy to settle for nothing less than her own soulmate.

as I shifted my perspective to believing in soulmates, I began to witness enduring love stories in amazing numbers.

Which world would you rather live in? If you want lasting love filled with happiness and joy wherever you look, begin to shift your perspective now. Look around for long-term happiness and affirm that you, too, can obtain it.

THE ROMANCE OF THE MUNDANE

Everyday life with your soulmate can be far more romantic than a brief fling, though in our culture the latter is more romanticized in movies and popular culture. Brushing your teeth with a person with whom you've built a life, shared so much, and forged such a deep connection seems much more romantic to me than a short, heated love affair.

Life is never stagnant. It moves forward, and in the grand scheme of things our time together on Earth is short. Each day we make a choice to be together, as well as numerous other choices that determine the course of our relationship. Each day we learn more secrets about one another, discover new facets to explore. As long as we choose love, honoring each other and growth together, things need not get dull. And as long as we remain grateful for our romantic partner, this gift from God, we will never be bored.

I think of all of the breakups and drama I never had with my husband and how much stronger this makes us. Bypassing the drama and diving into the depths takes you to places where you didn't know you could go. It opens up a whole new world, allowing other, far more enriching paths to be explored.

A WORLD OF LOVE

Your soulmate can be just the tip of the iceberg for you as far as love goes. I have always taught that you can live in a world where love is everywhere you look and each person you meet is simply new family. I never knew how true this could be until I met Jon, my husband, who is one of the most loving people I have ever known. He tends to attract love into his life because of his nature, and I continually marvel at the love that surrounds our lives. Since we have had children, we've been discovering a new and exotic world, as though people haven't been having kids throughout history. We often look over the heads of our children and marvel that we created these precious beings.

Your world will only grow richer as you walk through life with your beloved. This love strengthens you, making you more available for untold good. I believe that your heart opens to unprecedented degrees, and therefore has a greater capacity to both give love and receive love. Whatever magic is unleashed, keep opening to a world filled with love and joy. And you will find it.

I bless you on this wonderful journey into the arms of your love. I affirm that the desires of your heart were put there to propel you to their fulfillment. You are well on your way in the journey toward your soulmate and into a world that holds more love than you ever knew. What lies waiting for you is truly a Relationship from Heaven.

Appendix 1

A Ten-Week Soulmate Magnetization Program

(For Small Groups)

Why is it that you read an uplifting book like this one or go on a retreat and feel good for a few weeks only to fall back into old patterns of feeling less hopeful? Because after you finish the book or leave the retreat, it's easy to sit back and do nothing to perpetuate the transformation you had. You must work at staying positive. That is why I've included this Ten-Week Soulmate Magnetization Program, a way to use this book to keep you in a good, strong frame of mind even after you've finished reading the book. It makes what you have learned here sink in much deeper and shepherds you into embodying the truth outlined herein until you are in the arms of your One.

This book can be used for a ten-week study group, using one chapter as a guide each week. The value of participating in the group program is that you get the reinforcement of support in a group, and it increases your ability to apply this material to your own life. One of the principles of opening to your soulmate is staying in a good space, and this program helps you remain upbeat. The program is outlined below with specific instructions for each week. You will have weekly homework that includes reading the chapter at hand and doing an exercise or two. Each group time will include a structured agenda that should take you two to three hours, depending upon how many people are in your group. Schedule one meeting per week to get together.

I suggest that your group include no more than eight people to maximize your time.

GROUP RULES

If you are facilitating a group based on this material, you need to establish some ground rules for interaction. I use these guidelines in my workshops to keep everyone organized and positive. Read them out loud at the beginning of each meeting so that the group understands the guidelines for successful group interaction. If your group will share responsibility for leading each weekly meeting, the leader for the week can take on the responsibility of reading the rules before each meeting begins.

1. *Confidentiality.* What is said in this group remains in the group so that we all feel free to share without holding back. This means not only that we do not repeat what we hear in the group, but also that we don't even mention it if we see the person involved somewhere else unless they bring it up.

2. *No Advice Giving.* In this group, we don't presume to know what another person needs to do, so we don't give advice to anyone else here. If we have thoughts to share, we share from our own experience, what worked for us, instead of telling others what *they* should do.

3. *Supportiveness.* We are all cheerleaders for one another. We suspend judgment or negativity, and instead lift one another up, offering support and understanding.

4. *Participation.* We each commit to doing this work faithfully every week: the homework, sharing, and offering support to one another. If we have to miss a week, we still keep up with the work on our own and let someone know we have to skip a week. If we are late or have to leave early, we do so quietly, without disturbing the work in process.

I also suggest getting a timer that rings after a programmed amount of time to use when people are sharing. This makes sure everyone in the group, the quiet ones and the conversationalists alike, all get equal time to speak.

Also, decide if you'll take turns bringing refreshments and drinks or if you'll have a shared responsibility for doing so.

WEEK ONE: ERADICATING NEGATIVE THOUGHTS, BEGINNING TO BELIEVE IN YOUR ONE

Before the Meeting

- Make sure you get your own copy of this book (so

that you can mark it up and reread as necessary), a highlighter, and a blank notebook to use as your Soulmate Journal.

- Read the introduction and chapter 1, "Crackling Chemistry," highlighting anything that seems particularly important or that you have a question about.
- *Exercise 1:* On the first page of your Soulmate Journal, write down one sentence that you highlighted in your reading. Write a paragraph or two stating why this sentence resonated with you.
- *Exercise 2:* Do Magnetization Step 1: Dissolve Negative Thoughts and Let in Hope. Once you're finished, highlight one or two of the most important negative beliefs or hurts you've released along with the positive affirmations you wrote. You will share these with the group.

During the Meeting

First Fifteen Minutes: Greet one another, get drinks and snacks, find a place to sit, and settle in. Group members should sit in a circle. Make sure you have pens or pencils and some loose paper (Post-it notes will do) handy. Have a sheet of paper available for everyone to write down their name, e-mail address, and phone number so that you can compile a group contact sheet. Ask for a volunteer to copy the list and distribute it to everyone at the next meeting.

Opening: Have everyone hold hands around the circle, and ask one person to bless (out loud) your time together to love and each person's highest good. A simple blessing can be:

I bless this time together to the highest good for each group member. I bless it to love for all of us. Even now the magic begins.

Rules: Facilitator or host (if you're all sharing duties) can welcome everyone, state the week you're on (Week 1), and read the four rules for your time together (stated at the beginning of appendix 1).

Group Sharing: Because this is your first time together, you want to get to know one another. Each person should be given three minutes to introduce themselves. Go around the circle with each person speaking in turn, using your timer to regulate the time. When the timer goes off, the person speaking should finish up as quickly as possible. Try to use the whole time when you're speaking. Share the following with the group:

- Your name and what your connection to the group is
- Why you're here (a little deeper than just "my friend dragged me here")

Group Discussion: Have a fifteen- to twenty-minute discussion about the introduction and chapter 1 and how you feel about soulmates. Free-flow conversation is fine.

Break: When the timer goes off, take a bathroom break and reconvene in ten minutes.

Group Sharing: Go around the circle again and allow each person a turn to speak. Get out your Soulmate Journal. Each person may take two minutes to read one or two negative thoughts about love they've released along with the positive affirmation that replaces it.

Exercise: Once everyone has shared their negative thoughts and positive affirmations, each person in the group should write down the negative thoughts on a piece of paper. Bring out a trash can. Each person in turn should take his or her paper, rip it to shreds, and drop it into the wastebasket saying, "I now release my resistance to love." Those who are watching should support this process for each person by nodding and cheering them on. After everyone has taken a turn, put your hands on your hearts and proclaim together, "We are free and wide open to love."

Closing

If you have extra time, you can continue with open discussion, but before dismissing, hold hands and bless everyone home safe and sound and your week until you meet again. Simple blessings: "I bless us all for a wonderful week opening to love, and trust that we all get home safe and sound tonight."

WEEK TWO: SEND OUT A SOUL CALL

Before the Meeting

- Read chapter 2, "The Soul Call," highlighting anything that seems particularly important or that you have a question about.
- *Exercise:* Do Magnetization Step 2: Send Out a Soul Call, using your Soulmate Journal.

During the Meeting

First Fifteen Minutes: Greet one another, get drinks and snacks, find a place to sit, and settle in.

Opening: Have everyone hold hands around the circle, and ask one person to bless (out loud) your time together to love and each person's highest good. A simple blessing can be:

> I bless this time together to the highest good for each group member. I bless it to love for all of us. Even now the magic begins.

Rules: Facilitator or host (if you're all sharing duties) can welcome everyone, state the week you're on (Week 2), and read the four rules for your time together.

Group Sharing: Each person should be given three minutes to give a rundown of how their week went, with particular attention to their love life and being single. Those who are listening should be supportive.

Group Discussion: Have a fifteen- to twenty-minute discussion about chapter 2 and what it was like sending out your soul call as you did Magnetization Step 2.

Break: When the timer goes off, take a bathroom break and reconvene in ten minutes.

Group Sharing: Each person should be given two minutes to describe their soulmate, using the list they made in their journal. After the two minutes of describing his soulmate, once the timer has sounded, the person sharing should close his eyes, spread his arms wide, and proclaim out loud, "Soulmate, I welcome you into my life now." Those who are listening should also close their eyes and send their energetic support to the person speaking. After you welcome in your soulmate, take a moment to breathe in the energy before completing your turn.

Closing

If you have extra time, you can continue with open discussion, but before dismissing, hold hands and bless everyone home safe and sound and your week until you meet again. Simple blessings: "I bless us all for a wonderful week opening to love, and trust that we all get home safe and sound tonight."

WEEK THREE: HEALING YOUR FATAL FLAW, LETTING GO OF FEAR

Before the Meeting

- Read chapter 3, "He'll Run Screaming from the Room," highlighting anything that seems particularly important or that you have a question about.
- *Exercise:* Do Magnetization Step 3: Heal Your Fatal Flaw Belief, using your Soulmate Journal.

During the Meeting

First Fifteen Minutes: Greet one another, get drinks and snacks, find a place to sit, and settle in.

Opening: Have everyone hold hands around the circle, and ask one person to bless (out loud) your time together to love and each person's highest good. A simple blessing can be:

> I bless this time together to the highest good for each group member. I bless it to love for all of us. Even now the magic begins.

Rules: Facilitator or host (if you're all sharing duties) can welcome everyone, state the week you're on (Week 3), and read the four rules for your time together.

Group Sharing: Each person should be given three minutes to give a rundown of how their week went, with particular attention to their love life and being single. Those who are listening should be supportive.

Group Discussion: Have a fifteen- to twenty-minute discussion about the concept of the Fatal Flaw and insecurities about love.

Break: When the timer goes off, take a bathroom break and reconvene in ten minutes.

Group Sharing: Each person should be given three minutes to explain the Fatal Flaw they highlighted and how their exercise of releasing it went. Participants should be encouraged to show their Fatal Flaw to the group, if appropriate. Others in the group should be highly supportive. At the end of their turn, each participant should proclaim, "I now release my Fatal Flaw—[*state what it is*]—and know that I am lovable just as I am."

Closing

Before you close, remind everyone to do the Mirror Exercise from chapter 4 every day until you meet again. If you have extra time, you can continue with open discussion, but before dismissing, hold hands and bless everyone home safe and sound and your week until you meet again. Sample blessings: "I bless us all for a wonderful week opening to love, and trust that we all get home safe and sound tonight."

Note: In two weeks the group will have a guided meditation to do together. If you all want to participate and don't have a group facilitator, you can order the *Releasing a Person* CD or tape from the resources listed in appendix 2 so that everyone can participate. Otherwise, one person, the leader for the week, will need to read the meditation aloud and not participate in the meditation itself.

WEEK FOUR:
HOW WILL SHE KNOW YOU IF YOU'RE NOT YOU?

Before the Meeting

- Read chapter 4, "How Will She Know You if You're Not You?" highlighting anything that seems particularly important or that you have a question about.
- *Activity:* Every day until your group meets again, do the Mirror Exercise from this chapter. Note in your

Soulmate Journal how it feels and if it becomes different after you've done this exercise a few days.

- *Exercise:* Take the Insecurity Quiz in chapter 4. Write down anything you checked in your Soulmate Journal. Also do the Insecurity and Affirmation Exercise later in the chapter, recording your answers in your journal. Finally, do Magnetization Step 4: Find Out Who You Are, doing each part of the process completely.

During the Meeting

First Fifteen Minutes: Greet one another, get drinks and snacks, find a place to sit, and settle in.

Opening: Have everyone hold hands around the circle, and ask one person to bless (out loud) your time together to love and each person's highest good. A simple blessing can be: "I bless this time together to the highest good for each group member. I bless it to love for all of us. Even now the magic begins."

Rules: Facilitator or host (if you're all sharing duties) can welcome everyone, state the week you're on (Week 4), and read the four rules for your time together.

Group Sharing: Each person should be given three minutes to give a rundown of how their week went, with particular attention to their love life and being single. Those who are listening should be supportive.

Group Discussion: Have a fifteen- to twenty-minute discussion about being yourself and shining your light.

Break: When the timer goes off, take a bathroom break and reconvene in ten minutes.

Group Sharing: Each person should be given one minute to talk about their experience with the Mirror Exercise and how it felt. Once this is done, go back around the circle and allow each group member three minutes to read her affirmation from her journal from the Insecurity and Affirmation Exercise and to describe what she's learning about being herself.

Closing

If you have extra time, you can continue with open discussion, but before dismissing, hold hands and bless everyone home safe and sound and your week until you meet again. Sample blessings can be: "I bless us all for a wonderful week opening to love, and trust that we all get home safe and sound tonight."

Note: For next week's guided meditation, make sure you schedule the meeting at a place with plenty of room for the whole group to lie down. Everyone should also bring a pillow and blanket and a box of tissues.

WEEK FIVE: DECLUTTER YOUR HEART

Before the Meeting

- Read chapter 5, "Declutter Your Heart," on releasing

old loves, highlighting anything that seems particularly important or that you have a question about.

- *Exercise:* After you read this chapter, make a list in your Soulmate Journal of anyone you need to let go of. Write down why you need to release this person (or people). Also in your journal, write a letter to this person saying good-bye. (You won't send it.)

During the Meeting (Make sure there are tissues handy this time.)

First Fifteen Minutes: Greet one another, get drinks and snacks, find a place to sit, and settle in.

Opening: Have everyone hold hands around the circle, and ask one person to bless (out loud) your time together to love and each person's highest good. A simple blessing can be: "I bless this time together to the highest good for each group member. I bless it to love and also to release for all of us. Even now the magic begins."

Rules: Facilitator or host (if you're all sharing duties) can welcome everyone, state the week you're on (Week 5), and read the four rules for your time together.

Group Sharing: Each person should be given three minutes to give a rundown of how their week went, with particular attention to their love life and being single. Those who are listening should be supportive. (Be aware that some of you may have had a tough time this week, as releasing brings up much pain and may even trigger a call from your ex.)

Group Discussion: Have a fifteen- to twenty-minute discussion about chapter 5, and releasing old loves, being extra sensitive to the pain that may arise for some participants.

Break: When the timer goes off, take a bathroom break and reconvene in ten minutes.

Group Sharing: Each person should be given three minutes to talk about who they are releasing, why, and if they feel they have emotional healing to do that makes letting go difficult for them.

Guided Meditation: Everyone but the group facilitator or leader of the week should find a comfortable spot to lie down with their pillow and blanket (bring along some tissues in case they are needed). If you have the *Releasing a Person* CD or tape, the leader can cue it up to the "Guided Meditation" section and start it before lying down. This way everyone can participate. If you don't have the recording, the facilitator or leader of the week can read the release ritual from chapter 5. (The only difference is that you don't use the photo of your ex and close your eyes.) Experience the Release Meditation, going through each step as led. It is best to be lying down with your eyes closed. This meditation can bring up strong emotions, which is why it's good to have tissues with you.

After the Meditation: Take your time getting up after the guided meditation. If you need a hug, make sure to ask for one. No doubt others in the group will need a hug, too. Take some time before you all leave to support one another as needed.

Closing

If you have extra time, you can continue with open discussion, but before dismissing, hold hands and bless everyone home safe and sound and your week until you meet again. Sample blessings: "I bless us all for a wonderful week opening to love. I pronounce us all released and wide open to our soulmate. I trust that we all get home safe and sound tonight."

WEEK SIX: SHELTERING AND STRENGTHENING YOURSELF

Before the Meeting

- Read chapter 6, "A Delicate Time," highlighting anything that seems particularly important or that you have a question about.
- *Exercise:* After you read this chapter, make a list of people or situations in your life that are difficult for you emotionally. List your vulnerabilities. What triggers your feelings and why? Do Magnetization Step 6: Learn to Protect and Strengthen Yourself, writing down a few ways that you can shelter and strengthen yourself using the suggestions given. As instructed, complete three of these activities immediately and then each day until your meeting, continue to work on the list, creating a haven for your heart.

During the Meeting

First Fifteen Minutes: Greet one another, get drinks and snacks, find a place to sit, and settle in.

Opening: Have everyone hold hands around the circle, and ask one person to bless (out loud) your time together to love and each person's highest good. A simple blessing can be: "I bless this time together to the highest good for each group member. I bless it to love for all of us. Even now the magic begins."

Rules: Facilitator or host (if you're all sharing duties) can welcome everyone, state the week you're on (Week 6), and read the four rules for your time together.

Group Sharing: Each person should be given three minutes to give a rundown of how their week went, with particular attention to their love life and being single. Those who are listening should be supportive.

Group Discussion: Have a fifteen- to twenty-minute discussion about sheltering and strengthening yourself as you open to love.

Break: When the timer goes off, take a bathroom break and reconvene in ten minutes.

Group Sharing: Each person should be given three minutes to talk about what he or she finds emotionally difficult about being single. Participants can use the notes they've made in their journal as a guide (without reading straight from it, as you want to express yourself freely). After everyone has a turn, go back around the circle and allow each person one minute to share what he is going to do to shelter and fortify himself during this delicate time.

Exercise: Everyone should choose a partner and sit face-to-face for some role playing. Pretend your partner is someone who triggers negative feelings in you, perhaps someone who is particularly difficult for you to deal with. Tell your partner what this person says or does that triggers those negative feelings in you. Now spend five minutes interacting with this person in such a way that you protect yourself from negativity, using the suggestions in chapter 6. When the timer goes off, switch so that your partner has a chance to practice his or her defense techniques as well.

Closing

If you have extra time, you can continue with open discussion about this exercise. If a holiday is approaching, talk about your holiday plans and any ideas that will help you to have a good time. But before dismissing, hold hands and bless everyone home safe and sound and your week until you meet again. Sample blessings: "I bless us all for a wonderful week opening to love, and trust that we all get home safe and sound tonight."

WEEK SEVEN:
DISCOVERING YOUR OWN LOVE STYLE

Before the Meeting

- Read chapter 7, "Forget the One Hundred Frogs," highlighting anything that seems particularly important or that you have a question about.
- *Exercise:* Do Magnetization Step 7: Get in Touch with Your Love Style to get in touch with your own way of dating and connecting.

During the Meeting

First Fifteen Minutes: Greet one another, get drinks and snacks, find a place to sit, and settle in.

Opening: Have everyone hold hands around the circle, and ask one person to bless (out loud) your time together to love and each person's highest good. A simple blessing can be: "I bless this time together to the highest good for each group member. I bless it to love for all of us. Even now the magic begins."

Rules: Facilitator or host (if you're all sharing duties) can welcome everyone, state the week you're on (Week 7), and read the four rules for your time together.

Group Sharing: Each person should be given three minutes to give a rundown of how their week went, with particular attention to their love life and being single. Those who are listening should be supportive.

Group Discussion: Have a fifteen- to twenty-minute discussion about love styles and what you won't and don't have to do for love. Anyone who has a good "bad date" story can tell it now.

Break: When the timer goes off, take a bathroom break and reconvene in ten minutes.

Group Sharing: Each person should be given three minutes to talk about how they've forced themselves to get "out there" to date and even kiss people they don't particularly want to kiss. Talk about how you can act differently when you have the faith that your soulmate is on the way. What do you *want* to do as opposed to what you think you *should* do about your love life? Then go back around the circle and allow each person one minute to describe their own newly discovered love style.

Closing

If you have extra time, you can continue with open discussion about this exercise, and also discuss activities you enjoy that could lead to love. If anyone has a good story about people who met while staying at home, by all means they should share it. Before dismissing, hold hands and bless everyone home safe and sound and your week until you meet again. Sample blessings: "I bless us all for a wonderful week opening to love, and trust that we all get home safe and sound tonight."

WEEK EIGHT:
DISCOVERING A NEW WAY OF DATING

Before the Meeting

- Read chapter 8, "The Mating Dance," highlighting anything that seems particularly important or that you have a question about.
- *Exercise:* Do Magnetization Step 8: Make Dating Bearable, Even Fun to begin transforming your dating life.

During the Meeting

First Fifteen Minutes: Greet one another, get drinks and snacks, find a place to sit, and settle in.

Opening: Have everyone hold hands around the circle, and ask one person to bless (out loud) your time together to love and each person's highest good. A simple blessing can be: "I bless this time together to the highest good for each group member. I bless it to love for all of us. Even now the magic begins."

Rules: Facilitator or host (if you're all sharing duties) can welcome everyone, state the week you're on (Week 8), and read the four rules for your time together.

Group Sharing: Each person should be given three minutes to give a rundown of how their week went, with particular attention to their love life and being single. Those who are listening should be supportive.

Group Discussion: Have a fifteen- to twenty-minute discussion about chapter 8, Magnetization Step 8, and dating. Highlight any revelations that you had while reading the chapter, as well as anything you now realize you've been doing that hinders you.

Break: When the timer goes off, take a bathroom break and reconvene in ten minutes.

Group Sharing: Each person should be given three minutes to reveal the biggest mistakes they've made in dating so far and what they will do differently after reading this chapter.

Exercise: As a group, stand up. Circle your hips clockwise and then counterclockwise. Then thrust your hips forward, doing a pelvic thrust as you yell, "Uhh!" This may seem silly (feel free to laugh), but this exercise will help you to open your sexual energy. Now pair off and practice flirting with a partner. It may feel awkward, but pretend you're Mae West or Pepé Le Pew. Have fun with it. It doesn't matter if you and your partner are the same gender and you're not gay—flirt anyway. Do this with a few partners, as time permits. Vow to find your own brand of flirting, be it subtle or obvious.

Closing

Before dismissing, hold hands and bless everyone home safe and sound and your week until you meet again. Sample blessings: "I bless us all for a wonderful week opening to love, and trust that we all get home safe and sound tonight."

WEEK NINE: COUNTDOWN TO LOVE LIFTOFF

Before the Meeting

- Read chapter 9, "Countdown to Love Liftoff," on getting ready for love, highlighting anything that seems particularly important or that you have a question about.
- *Exercise 1:* Do Magnetization Step 9: Prepare for the Ride of Your Life, recording the different lists in your Soulmate Journal.
- *Exercise 2:* Before the week is up, go out alone using the Learn to Be Alone Exercise in chapter 9 as your guide. Record in your Soulmate Journal how difficult or easy this experience was for you.

During the Meeting

First Fifteen Minutes: Greet one another, get drinks and snacks, find a place to sit, and settle in.

Opening: Have everyone hold hands around the circle, and ask one person to bless (out loud) your time together to love and each person's highest good. A simple blessing can be: "I bless this time together to the highest good for each group member. I bless it to love for all of us. Even now the magic begins."

Rules: Facilitator or host (if you're all sharing duties) can welcome everyone, state the week you're on (Week 9), and read the four rules for your time together.

Group Sharing: Each person should be given three minutes to give a rundown of how their week went, with particular attention to their love life and being single. Those who are listening should be supportive.

Group Discussion: Have a fifteen- to twenty-minute discussion about how you are getting ready for love. Discuss patience in general and how it can pay off for you. Who is good at going places alone, and who isn't? How deep is your faith that love is yours?

Break: When the timer goes off, take a bathroom break and reconvene in ten minutes.

Group Sharing: Each person should be given three minutes to reveal his or her patience level concerning love right now. Also share some ideas from your list that you want or need to do before love knocks on your door.

Closing

If you have extra time, discuss ways to keep yourself in a positive frame of mind as you open to love. Before dismissing, hold hands and bless everyone home safe and sound and your week until you meet again. Sample blessings: "I bless us all for a wonderful week opening to love, and trust that we all get home safe and sound tonight."

Note: For next week's graduation ceremony, enlist someone to bring flowers as well as other fun tokens (eg., crowns, fake wedding rings) for each person in the group. Plan your graduation party to be a joyful celebration of the work you've done.

WEEK TEN: ONCE IT'S HAPPENED

Before the Meeting

- Read chapter 10, "Once It's Happened," on the Relationship from Heaven, highlighting anything that seems particularly important or that you have a question about.
- *Exercise:* After you read this chapter, jot down in your Soulmate Journal the challenges you have had in relationships so far. Are you an arguer? Do control or money issues tend to come up in your relationships? Write down everything that has been difficult for you in a love union. What caused your breakups? Now write down everything you want in your ideal relationship.

During the Meeting

First Fifteen Minutes: Greet one another, get drinks and snacks, find a place to sit, and settle in.

Opening: Have everyone hold hands around the circle, and ask one person to bless (out loud) your time together to love and each person's highest good. A simple blessing can be: "I bless this time together to the highest good for each group member. I bless it to love for all of us. Even now the magic begins. I am so grateful we've had this time together, and trust that this, our last meeting, holds many gifts."

Rules: Facilitator or host (if you're all sharing duties) can welcome everyone, state the week you're on (Week 10), and read the four rules for your time together.

Group Sharing: Each person should be given three minutes to give a rundown of how their week went, with particular attention to their love life and being single. Those who are listening should be supportive.

Group Discussion: Have a fifteen- to twenty-minute discussion about the Relationship from Heaven. Discuss the ideas you've had about relationships that may have limited you. What has come up for you that has been difficult? Participants should be encouraged to share examples of any happily married couples they know and describe those relationships.

Break: When the timer goes off, take a bathroom break and reconvene in ten minutes.

Group Sharing: Each person should be given three minutes to share the problems they've had in relationships so far and what their ideal relationship looks like.

Exercise: Go around the room and have each person share in *only one or two sentences* what limited idea about relationships they are ready to release. Then go back around the room, having each person state, "I, *[participant's name]* , now release my idea that relationships are ____________________." After each person makes their statement, the rest of the group should say with conviction, "Done!"

Extra Activity: If you have extra time, discuss ways you can improve your communication by using the Levels of Communication and Fair Fight Rules listed in chapter 10.

Graduation Ceremony and Party

In celebration of your graduation, one at a time have each person go into the center of the circle and proclaim, "I am wide open and ready for love. My One is coming to me." After making this proclamation, each person should be given a flower, be crowned, or participate in some other brief ritual to symbolize his or her graduation. The group should clap for each graduate before the next one steps into the circle. After everyone has been recognized with this ceremony, close your time together by holding hands, blessing this next phase of your journey to love and blessing you all home safe and sound. Sample blessings: "I bless us all for successfully completing this journey and affirm that love is on its way to each of us. Before we know it, we are in the arms of our soulmates, living in a world of love and connection. Already, this sacred process has begun. I trust that we all get home safe and sound tonight and sleep in the arms of angels."

After the closing, invite everyone to eat, have dessert, and celebrate together how far you've come.

CONTINUING THE PROGRAM

I find that when you begin a group like the one I've described here, you bond to such an extent that you don't want the experience to end. And it doesn't have to. You can continue this work together very easily for as long as you like, and the consistent support is extremely helpful as you journey onward. The format of the meetings can be the same. As you may have noticed, the activities are generally the same for each week, other than the homework and the last part of the meeting.

What I suggest is to follow the burning issue each week. When you participate in a group, you become extremely connected, and you will find that many of you have the same problems or concerns come up at the same time in your lives. Explore these parallels together during your group time. You may use the topics suggested in the book, but if something beyond that comes up, explore it together. As some of you eventually experience the joy of connecting with your soulmates, you will want to focus on chapter 10. Whatever you are dealing with, go back to the chapter that addresses it, reread parts that apply, and record in your Soulmate Journal what you are going through as well as what you can do about it, using suggestions from the book.

For the final exercise each week, each person can spend three minutes sharing not only what he is up against, but also what he is doing about the situation to make it better.

Blessings upon you as you continue this work. I support you and trust that you will manifest your heart's desire—the lasting love that makes your heart sing.

Appendix 2

Recommended Resources

The following books and recordings will help you keep your energy in a good place and your spirits high.

A Gift of Love: Marriage as a Spiritual Journey, by Ann Tremaine Linthorst (New York: Paulist Press, 1979). This book is a marriage and relationship saver. It outlines a better way to conduct a relationship, be it with your love, your family, or your friends.

Getting the Love You Want: A Guide for Couples, by Harville Hendrix (New York: Henry Holt, 1988). If you still have childhood issues that need healing, this is one of the best books you can read to aid in your healing process. It also will help you to understand your partner and forge a better relationship.

God on a Harley:A Spiritual Fable (New York: Pocket Books, 1995) and *Heaven in High Gear* (Thorndike, ME. G. K. Hall, 1998), by Joan Brady. These two fictional tales offer a new way to look at yourself and at love, while being quite entertaining. And yes, Jesus shows up on a motorcycle.

Manifesting Love: Call Forth Your Soulmate with This Powerful Process, by Kathryn Alice. (The Alice Tompkins Company, 2004) This recording takes you through the soul call, especially the part where you welcome love in on the inner through a guided process.

Releasing a Person: Recover from a Breakup or Divorce, by Kathryn Alice. (The Alice Tompkins Company, 2003) This recording takes you through the steps that I teach to let go. Most valuable is the guided meditation in which you do an actual effective release, something you can use in your group program as well.

Single in the City E-zine, by Kathryn Alice. This free, twice-monthly e-zine is intended to help keep your thoughts positive as you open to love. Subscribe at www.KathrynAlice.com. You will automatically be subscribed once you join our mailing list.

Soulmates and Twin Flames: The Spiritual Dimension of Love and Relationships, by Elizabeth Clare Prophet (Corwin Springs, MT: Summit University Press, 1999). A small, interesting book on the concept of your ultimate soulmate.

The Four Agreements: A Practical Guide to Personal Freedom, by Don Miguel Ruiz (San Rafael, CA: Amber-Allen, 1997). I recommend this book in chapter 10, and it is one of the best treatises on learning not to take things personally that I have ever encountered.

The Mastery of Love: A Practical Guide to the Art of Relationship, by Don Miguel Ruiz (San Rafael, CA: Amber-Allen, 1999). This book is extremely valuable in helping you emotionally heal. It gives you a picture of how you got damaged in the first place and how to get better.

The Power of Now: A Guide to Spiritual Enlightenment, by Eckhart Tolle (Novato, CA: New World Library, 1999). If you have emotional healing to do, the chapter in this book on the pain body is not to be missed. Also especially valuable is the chapter on relationships.

Twin Souls: Finding Your True Spiritual Partner, by Patricia Joudry and Maurie D. Pressman, MD (New York: Carol Southern Books, 1995). Want to find out more about the twin soul/twin flame concept (your ultimate soulmate)? This is the best book I've found on the subject, and it is quite inspiring.

For other resources, support and articles, visit my Web site: www.KathrynAlice.com.

Endnotes

1. Press Release from the Public Information Office of the United States Department of Commerce, Census Bureau, June 29, 2001.
2. Ayala Malach Pines, *Falling in Love: Why We Choose the Lovers We Choose* (New York: Routledge, 1999).
3. D. Cichetti, S. L. Toth, and Hennesy, *Topics in Early Childhood Special Education.*
4. David L. Weiner, *Reality Check: What Your Mind Knows But Isn't Telling You* (New York: Prometheus Books, 2005).
5. Ibid.
6. "Power of Positive Thinking May Have a Health Benefit, Study Says," *New York Times* (September 2, 2003).
7. About.com., *Stress Management: The Benefits of Optimism*, May 2006. http://stress.about.com/od/optimismspirituality/a/optimismbenefit.htm.
8. Pines, *Falling in Love.*
9. Helen E. Fisher, *Anatomy of Love* (New York: Ballantine, 1994).
10. Richard W. Robins and K. H. Trzesniewski, "Self-Esteem Development Across the Lifespan," *Current Directions in Psychological Science* 14, no.3, pp. 158–62.
11. University of Michigan Press Release, "Study Finds Happiness Persists, Despite Illness" (February 10, 2005).
12. Norman Cousins, *Anatomy of an Illness as Perceived by the Patient: Reflections on Healing and Regeneration* (New York: W. W. Norton and Company, 1979).
13. Herbert Benson, MD, and Miriam Z. Klipper, *The Relaxation Response* (New York: William Morrow and Co., 1975).

Index